THE BOOK OF BLANDFORD FORUM

Blandford Market Place about 1850. (BM)

Blandford from the East. (DWIA)

THE BOOK OF BLANDFORD FORUM

The story of the town's past

BY

BENJAMIN G. COX

DORSET BOOKS

The Book of Blandford Forum was originally published in 1984 by Barracuda Books Ltd and this edition is reproduced by permission of Quotes Ltd, publishers of the The Barracuda Collection.

Republished 1993 by Dorset Books

British Library Cataloguing in Publication Data
CIP Catalogue Record for this book
is available from the British Library

ISBN: 1 871164 17 6

DORSET BOOKS

Official Publisher to Dorset County Council
1 Chinon Court
Lower Moor Way
TIVERTON EX16 6SS

Tel: 0884 243242
Fax: 0884 243325

Printed and bound in Great Britain by Bookcraft, Midsomer Norton

Contents

Author's Note to the 1993 Edition

I was pleased to be invited to agree to a reprint of *The Book of Blandford Forum* as I knew that, as a basic history of the town, it required nothing much in the way of correction. Research has since revealed that a church existed in the town between 1101 and 1118. Most of the research carried out since 1984 has been made the subject of local history monographs published by the Blandford Forum Museum Trust and should be read as supplementary to *The Book of Blandford Forum.*

Benjamin G. Cox
August 1993

Acknowledgements

I would like to place on record the considerable help I have received from fellow members of the Blandford Forum Museum Trust, from many Blandford residents, from Mrs S. Fry ALA, and staff at Blandford Public Library who have rendered me a first class service, from Miss M. Holmes MA, until recently county archivist at Dorchester and the staff of the County Record Office, from Mr R. N. R. Peers MA FSA AMA, and staff at Dorchester County Museum, The British Library, The Public Records Office and other bodies holding archives and records of Blandford. I have also been saved considerable research by the courtesy of Mrs Joy Adams, who made available to me the records kept by her late husband, and my friend, Mr Victor J. Adams, who died in March 1983.

My thanks are also due to many people including Mr & Mrs S. Jardine for their considerable help in looking out old photographs and supplying information from their files, to the Blandford Forum Museum Trust and the Blandford Town Council for permission to reproduce photographs from their collections, and to all others who have allowed me to use photographs in their possession taken by photographers of days gone by who cannot now be identified.

I have supplemented my own researches by reference to the publications by and scholarship of Blandford historians of the past – any differences of opinion expressed by me arise largely on account of new information coming to light as the result of more recent research.

In this brief record of the town's past, I am conscious that many aspects have not been touched upon and others dealt with only briefly. I have made little reference to Blandford St Mary as this has been so adequately documented by Miss T. F. Almack in her *A Village Heritage* published in 1961. Bryanston is to be the subject of a separate work by me at a later date. I hope I have made the best of the space allowed and that I have left sufficient scope for someone to write a more detailed account of the last 150 years or so which I necessarily have had to skip over fairly lightly.

Preface

by Peter J. Reynolds, MA PhD FSA MIFA
Director, Butser Ancient Farm Project Trust

It is both a privilege and a pleasure to be invited to write the preface to this *Book of Blandford Forum* especially so since the author has been a friend and colleague for over twenty years. It is in the early years of one's professional career that the influences received are critical, and it was my good fortune to meet and work under and with the author of this volume. From him I learned the value and fascination of detail on the one hand, on the other how to vest that detail with the 'red meat' of local history. In Worcestershire, especially in the Vale of Evesham, 'Ben' Cox made an outstanding contribution as an historian, museum curator and archaeologist. His enthusiasm and selfless devotion was instrumental not only in setting up the Almonry Museum in Evesham, thus giving the town back its missing heritage, but also in organising, inspiring and driving to fruition the publication *The Research Papers,* a biennial publication of which I happened to be the first editor. His many published works relating to that area are of fundamental importance to researchers, students of local history and the general public. The 'Book of Evesham' and 'Yesterday's Town — Evesham' were, and still are, extremely successful publications. Thus it is that Worcestershire's loss of a scholar can now be counted as Blandford's gain. The *Book of Blandford Forum* similarly is at once a scholarly treatise and a highly readable storehouse of information. The material is treated with singular sympathy and understanding and it is a book which will have a far wider appeal than the narrow confines its title suggests.

Peter J. Reynolds

Foreword

by Councillor D. H. Davies, MRCS LRCP

Mr Ben Cox is a relative newcomer to Blandford, but in a short space of time, he has become a highly valued member of our community.

He is the Founder Curator of our newly established Town Museum, where the visitor will find ample evidence of his scholarship and expertise. These two qualities are equally well reflected in this, *The Book of Blandford Forum*, which not only satisfies a long felt local need, but will give pleasure to the many world-wide who hold Blandford in high esteem and affection, be they exiles from their native heath, members of the Armed Forces who have served in our locality or ex-pupils of our neighbouring schools.

The story, deeply researched and succinctly narrated is eminently readable and presented in such a way as to increase its fascination and compass.

The history of Blandford is, of necessity, in many ways the history of England, but certain Blandfordian characteristics, notably a sturdy independence and fierce local pride, have given variations from the general national historical theme.

The appearance of *The Book of Blandford Forum* at this juncture in our Town's history is particularly apt, as during this decade our population may well double, and adopted Blandfordians like myself will, in the light of the knowledge of our Town's history, share that pride held by those privileged to have Blandford as their birth place.

I strongly recommend this book, particularly to our children, so that they may grow up in the knowledge that they are citizens of no mean Town.

D. H. Davies

Blandford Appraised

A few extracts from recorded impressions of Blandford by eminent persons and diarists.

1630s A faire markett towne, pleasantlie seated upon the river and neare unto the downs, well inhabitted and of goode traffique.

Thomas Gerrard of Trent

1640 Blandford was the most eminent schoole for the education of gentlemen in the West of England. At Blandford as much roguery as at Newgate.

John Aubrey, a past pupil

1669 We came to Blandford, a little town of four thousand souls, situated in a small valley watered by the river Stour. His highness was saluted by the ringing of bells, which piece of respect was shewed at all the places he met with on the road.

Count Lorenzo Magalotti
(Travels of Cosmo III, Grand Duke of Tuscany)

1680 From thence (Wilton) I went to Blandford in Dorsetshire through a haire waring (hare warren) and a forest of the kings (Cranborne Chase). Blandford is a pretty neate country town.

Celia Fiennes (The Journeys)

1724 Blandford is a flourishing borough and market town containing 500 houses, many of them built of stone. It is a thoroughfare on the coach road to Exeter. No town hereabouts has so great a number of gentlemens seats round about it as this, invited hither perhaps by the pleasant downs adjoining which can hardly be equalled in the world. It is now one of the most considerable towns of the county for travellers.

Daniel Defoe

1754 There are many good inns and shops in the town and they have a considerable trade in malt; it is a great thorough fare to the west. They have a very handsome church of hewn stone, built by the contributions after the fire.

Dr Richard Pococke

1760 Lunched at the Greyhound in Blandford; 'tis well built and populous, more so indeed as it was their fair and visitation time. I've heard that formerly 'twas the greatest manufactory in England of bone lace, but what is remarkable is that the poorer sort of its present inhabitants told us they never knew that it was ever so.

Mrs Phillip Lybbe Powys

1760 Our stay at Blandford was very agreable, the weather fine. The gentlemen of the county shewed us great hospitality particularly Messrs. Portman, Pleydell, Bower, Sturt, Brain, Jennings, Drax and Trenchard, but partly thro' their fault and partly thro' ours their hospitality was often debauch.

Edward Gibbon,
author of Decline & Fall of the Roman Empire.
Written when he was 23 and a captain
in the Hampshire militia.

1788 Passing through the village of Whitchurch we come to a long range of bleak hills and downs, which brings us suddenly upon the pleasant town of Blandford. From here we have a delightful view of Brianston the elegant mansion of Mr Portman. Blandford is a borough town and being burnt down in 1731 rose like another phoenix from the ashes with the handsome plumage it now wears.

Rev Stebbing Shaw

1791 We heard the service performed very well at Blandford church which is a very pretty edifice of late date, built after the old one, with the whole town, about a century ago. After an early dinner we set off for Milton Abbey the seat of Lord Milton.

Fanny Burney

1791 By eleven at night we drove up to the Greyhound at Blandford; and the next morning were much gratified with the sight of the full market place directly under our windows. I was told that some hundreds, perhaps thousands of women and children here are employed in a manufacture of shirt buttons.

John O'Keefe, the dramatist

1798 Blandford, our next stage, lies about sixteen miles from Dorchester, and, though not a place of much renouned antiquity, is still perhaps a still more agreable town, and is pleasantly seated among meadows and woods. If a person wished to retire from business, where he might have the conveniences and pleasures of the town and country united, his choice might waver between Barnstable, Dorchester and Blandford. If he loved meadows and woodlands, he must make choice of Blandford.

Rev William Gilpin

1799 At the entrance (to Blandford) there is an old farmhouse still retaining a monastic appearance (possibly the chapel of St. Leonard). The streets are spacious and well built: some of them are paved with freestone.

George Lipscombe

Salisbury Street about 1895. (BM)

LEFT: Mousterian hand-axe from Handley Common; (MG) RIGHT: flint axe-head from Stourpaine c2500 BC; (BM) CENTRE: part of polished flint axe from Ash Oaks Farm, Stourpaine, (BM) and BELOW: Bronze-age palstave from Stourpaine c1300 BC. (BM)

Blaen-y-Ford

Who was the first man to walk into Blandford? We can only guess, but we can safely assume that he was a hunter and that he probably came here in the Mousterian (Middle Palaeolithic) period of pre-history between 40,000 and 75,000 years ago. Very few artefacts of this period have ever been found in Dorset, the nearest so far being a hand-axe found at Handley Common. If anything was left behind in Blandford it has still to be found. He may have come just to cross the river, as Blandford came into being due to its situation at the junction of several trackways leading from the surrounding downlands to a major crossing place over the Stour.

About 6,000 to 8,000 years ago, towards the end of the Mesolithic period, the people of Dorset were cut off from the mainland of Europe by the submergence of land now beneath the English channel. Over the centuries they were invaded by, and intermixed with, other tribes who came over from the continent. They were largely nomadic and their various cultures made up the Neolithic or New Stone Age. They made tools and weapons of stone, ivory and bone, the later stone artefacts being ground and polished. They buried some of their dead in long barrows, the one at Pimperne being a good example. Some of these later tribes came from Germany and Holland in about 2,000 BC and brought with them a new type of pottery earning them the name 'the beaker people'. Later still, others came, bringing with them weapons, utensils and personal ornaments of bronze. These early Bronze Age men took over gradually, as did most new cultures in pre-history, and they would have been here about 1800 BC their artefacts becoming more sophisticated as time went on. Finds of this period can be seen in local museums at Dorchester, Wimborne, Shaftesbury and Blandford. Their numerous round barrows, like the long ones of the neolithic period, can easily be found by field walking and reference to ordnance sheets. They give a clue to the general areas of local settlement but archaeologists have not yet succeeded in producing satisfactory evidence of permanent settlement sites.

The next major culture, very much in evidence in the Blandford area, is that of the Iron Age, commencing about 550 BC and the culture which the Roman armies found when they finally invaded

England in AD 43. The people living here then were in the tribal territory of the Durotriges, which comprised Dorset and fringes of adjoining counties. They were largely a farming community and remained so throughout the Roman occupation. Finds of the coins of the Durotriges in this area indicate that trade other than barter was carried on. These people lived mostly in the hill forts and hill-top enclosures at Busbury, Badbury, Hambledon, Hod, Rawlesbury and Spetisbury but, with their livestock, spent much of their lives, in times of peace, in the valleys below. These Iron Age men of Dorset were overcome by the Second 'Augusta' legion of the Roman army under the command of Vespasian, who was later to become emperor. He had to overcome resistance at over 20 of these hillforts in Dorset. Fierce fighting took place at Badbury Rings, Maiden Castle and Hod Hill, where a large quantity of balista bolts have been found. The Romans constructed their own fortress on Hod Hill in order to more easily keep down any local resistance, and occupied the site for about ten years after the invasion.

There is no evidence of Blandford itself having been occupied, in the sense that it was lived in, in Romano-British times, but the possibility of future finds cannot be ruled out. Considerable evidence exists of settlement sites in the Stour valley, including those at Stourpaine, Blandford St Mary and Bryanston. Major villas, farms and centres of activity have been excavated at Tarrant Hinton, Iwerne Minster, Hemsworth, Dewlish and elsewhere. There was a major road junction near Badbury Rings and the possibility of an important Roman station in the area. Relying on various lists of posting stations made by the Romans themselves, and by others in the late seventh century Ravenna itinerary, archaeologists believe this place to have been the one listed as Vindogladia. There are considerable doubts as to its precise location and these will only be cleared up by excavation. Vindogladia is a latinised version of a Celtic term meaning 'white ditches' which certainly applies to Badbury rings. The suggestion that Blandford Forum was the site of a Roman place called Iberium can be discounted. The extensive excavations carried out by General Pitt-Rivers at Iwerne Minster in 1879, revealing a major villa settlement, indicate that this was more likely to be Iberium – the name of the place is not so different to the present-day Iwerne. Blandford did not have 'Forum' added to its name until mediaeval times.

The Romano-British settlements in the Blandford area were all linked by secondary roads and tracks to the principal Roman highway, running from Old Sarum to Dorchester via Badbury rings. The way of life of the people living in these settlements was little changed by the coming of the Romans. The main advantages to the natives, living outside the towns, was that they were presented with better opportunities for trade, could enjoy the many luxury goods imported from the continent, such as pottery of a finer quality than their own native wares, artefacts of glass, silver, gold and bronze and ornaments, jewellery and perfumes for the ladies. They also benefited from the stable form of government, the Roman monetary system and, by the fourth century, from the introduction of Christianity. The numerous Roman coins found in the Stour valley over the years indicate a considerable trade. The Roman administration encouraged the local farmers to produce more food to help feed their armies here and abroad.

After the Roman occupation ended in the early fifth century, life went on much the same in the Blandford area for another 150 years or so. Resistance to Saxon invasions was strong in Dorset, and they were kept out for a good deal longer than was the case in many other parts of the west country. Bokerly Dyke, the six-mile-long earthwork bisecting the main road constructed from Salisbury to Dorchester, on the county boundary a few miles north of Blandford, and dated by General Pitt-Rivers as being of the late Roman period, was rebuilt and strengthened as part of these defences. It was not until the middle of the seventh century that the Saxon hordes were able to break through and over-run the county, which eventually became absorbed into their Kingdom of Wessex. No structure, artefact or other evidence of Saxon occupation has ever been identified in Blandford Forum itself, and one can assume from this that during most of the Anglo-Saxon period the place had no more than a few dwellings of timber construction with thatched roofing much as one would have found here at any time in the prevous 1,000 years or more.

At some time in the next 300 years or so, the general area of the town on both sides of the river, north, south, east and west, had become known as Blaen-y-ford or 'the place in front of the ford'. Nine estates or manors, each bearing the name 'Bleneford' or 'Blaneford' are shown in the Domesday survey of Dorset made in 1085/6. These were subsequently absorbed into and became part of the present parishes of Blandford Forum, Blandford Saint Mary, Bryanston and Langton Long Blandford. They were mostly estates held of the King by Robert, Count of Mortain, who held about 70 other manors in Dorset, William de Eu, Roger Arundel, Aiulf the chamberlain, Dodeman, 'the land of the king's thanes', which was land held by Englishmen, and 'the land of Ulviet'. The survey also gives the names of the local pre-conquest holders of some of these estates, including Edmer, Bretel, Sared and his brother and Alward. The concensus of opinion is that the manor now identified as Blandford Forum, was the demesne of Robert, Count of Mortain. The precise location within the local parishes of the other manors has not yet been positively proved and there will be no attempt here to add to the many opinions put forward. None of these manors had attained urban status at the time of the survey.

The entry relating to Blandford Forum is translated as follows: 'The count himself holds Bleneford. Edmer held it T.R.E. (at the time of King Edward) and it paid geld for 10 hides. There is land for 6 ploughs. In demesne there are 3 ploughs and 8 serfs and 7 villeins and 9 bordars with 2 ploughs. There is a mill rendering 20 shillings and 20 acres of meadow. Pasture 9 furlongs long and 3 furlongs wide. 5½ furlongs of woodland. It was worth £10=now £11.'

The other Blenefords adopted additions to their names over the years. Some of them combined to become Blandford Parva and came into the hands of the Martel family. When William Martel, as lord of this manor, gave a large part of it to the nunnery of St Mary Clerkenwell in 1152, a new manor was created. The land given to the church became Blandford Marie and the remainder Blandford Martel. All eventually became known as Blandford St Mary. At the time of King John, the Blaneford which we now know as Bryanston, was held by Bryan de Insula, a loyal supporter of the King. It became Blaneford Bryan and later Bryanston. Langton Long Blaneford was most likely so named because of its shape.

By 1150 that part of the town which is now central Blandford Forum had taken on a different identity to the remaining estates and had become urbanised. In 1190 it formed part of a group of manors known as The Honour of Leicester having been granted in that year by Richard I to Robert Fitzparnel, Earl of Leicester. The Earl died in 1204 without an heir to his earldom and his estates passed temporarily to his sisters, Amicia who married Simon de Montfort the second and Margaret who married Saier de Quincy, Earl of Winchester.

When King John visited Blandford in 1216 markets were already being held and a precept was directed to the Sheriff of Dorset ordering that markets should thereafter be held on Saturdays instead of Sundays. It was commonplace for markets to be held in close proximity to churches.

The Earldom of Leicester was recreated in 1239 when Amicia's grandson, Simon de Montfort the fourth, was given the title and estates. This Simon de Montfort is regarded as the father of parliamentary democracy in England and was the champion of the barons in their fight against his brother-in-law, Henry III. Simon was killed and his army routed at the battle of Evesham in 1265 and his estates reverted to the King. These manors of the former Honour of Leicester were subsequently granted to Henry de Lacy, who became Earl of Lincoln in 1272. Blandford Forum was shortly after described as his 'free borough belonging to the manor of Kingston Lacy with gallows, pillory, tumbrel, a market on Saturdays and a fair on the vigil of St. Simon and St. Jude and fifteen days following'.

Trade in Blandford was stimulated by the building of a bridge over the Stour to take the traffic in and out of the town in the Dorchester direction. This was most likely to have been of wooden construction; it was first noted in 1278 as 'pons de Blaneford' but was probably there much earlier.

The Borough was given a variety of names in the 13th century, including, with variations of spelling, Blaneford Forum, Blaneford-super-Stur (1279) and Cheping Blaneford (1288). The parliamentary writs for 1304 show Nicholas de Holt and Nicholas Horne as representing the Borough. The only subsequent occasion when Blandford was represented in its own right was in 1348/9, when Ralph de Usher and Roger de Manynford attended. Numerous attempts were made in subsequent centuries to secure for the borough a seat in Parliament, but without success.

In response to a petition made to Henry I in 1306/7, Henry de Lacy was granted the right to hold another annual fair 'in his vill of Blaneford on the vigil day and feast of the apostles Peter and Paul'. It is also recorded at this time that his 'free burgesses', ie those who were not required to perform any services to the manor and were almost freeholders, were paying between them forty shillings a year by way of rents.

The Dorset Lay Subsidy Roll of 1332 names the principal residents in Blandford Forum liable to pay taxes and includes Nicholas Horne, previously mentioned:

Johanne Welywat	Johanne le Webbe
Galfrido Burgys	Willelmo Forthonk
Edwardo de Burgh	Willelmo Bak
Thoma Todd	Nicholas Horn
Johanne Weke	Thoma Hert
Roberto Tanner	Johanne Kyng
Adam Skynner	Johanne Skynner
Ricardo le Clerk	Thomas Bal
Johanne Tanner	Willelmo Basset

Johanne Quarel.

By 1331 Henry de Lacy had died. The patent rolls of Edward I (vol 1 p 336) read 'Presentation of William de Nottele, Chaplain, to the church of Blaneford Chepying' on the death 'of Henry de Lacy, late Earl of Lincoln, being in his hands'. Henry de Lacy's estates were then granted to Henry Bolingbroke, Duke of Lancaster, a son of John of Gaunt, as tenant in chief, with the earldoms of Derby, Lincoln and Leicester. On Henry of Lancaster becoming Henry IV in 1399, the borough became a parcel of the Duchy of Lancaster and, as such, Crown lands. The borough then adopted the heraldic arms of the Duchy of Lancaster which are: 'Gules, 3 lions per pale passant, gardant, in chief of label of 3 points or'. The borough seal bears the legend 'Sigillum Berguntium Villae de Blanford Forum' around the arms of the Duchy. The small 'd' in the middle of Blandford only became standard about 200 years ago. Many Blandfordians still omit the middle 'd' when referring to the town in conversation.

The Black Death, which is reputed to have entered England via Melcome Regis in July 1348, spread rapidly throughout the country and no doubt Blandford suffered its share of deaths.

As many Borough and parish records were lost or destroyed in the 18th and 19th centuries, not many pre-census lists exist to tell us the surnames of the old Blandford families. We are, however, fortunate in having the Dorset Tudor subsidy rolls for 1525/93 and the Tudor muster rolls for 1542. The subsidy rolls show who was liable to taxation and the muster rolls list the able-bodied men between the ages of 15 and 60 available for military service, and the equipment available to each. Population experts have deduced from these returns that the population of Blandford borough was then well under 1,000.

When John Leland made his itinerary of Dorset for Henry VIII between 1535 and 1543, he had little to say about Blandford, beyond that it belonged to the Duchy of Lancaster and that there was a bridge. Nothing was noted about the buildings, the market or the church, as one might have expected. Perhaps he was not well received. He did note that John Ryves, the principal resident at the time, was 'a great heyne in Blandford'. A 'heyne' is generally understood to mean a miserly sort of person.

In 1591 the Duchy of Lancaster caused a survey to be made of its estates in Blandford, and the burgage holders in the borough who paid quit rents were named as:

Thomas Godderd	William Olyver
Richard Swayne	John Bremble
Christopher Comedge	Thomas Meade
Richard Ryves	Edward Machem
Richard Chapman	Robert Harben
Thomas Kinge	The heirs of Wm. Kinge

The heirs of Roger Newburroge

The survey also confirmed the bounds of the Borough and, on checking this with a Government report on the Borough made in 1832, it is clear that they had remained unchanged in the interim. The 1832 report is the easier to follow now and reads as follows: 'From the bridge over the River Stower on the road leading to Dorchester the boundary line runs for a very short distance to the westward; it then turns to the north and continues in a northern direction in Mr Portman's grounds, then turns eastwards into the street and runs along the West side of the street following the line of street by the Crown Inn and all the houses on the west side of the street. The line diverges from Salisbury street at a point where several streets meet, and takes an easterly direction until it crosses Damary Lane; it then goes southward on the east side of Damary Lane until it joins the road leading to Langton when it takes a westward direction and forms a waving line as far as a field called The Marsh; it then turns to the south, crosses the River Stower, and runs along the south bank of the river in a westerly direction until it again joins the bridge upon the Dorchester road'.

This remained the Borough limits until the 1899 extensions came into force.

By the end of the first Elizabeth's reign the markets and fairs of the Borough had achieved considerable fame and the town had attracted a number of wealthy private residents and merchants. It supported its own grammar school and almshouses and accommodated the registry of the Archdeacon of Dorset, then under the diocese of Bristol. Its affairs were conducted by a Common Council comprising a steward appointed by the Duchy of Lancaster, a bailiff who was head of the Council and ten leaders of the town who called themselves, at different times, 'the common council' or 'the capital burgesses'. They filled vacancies themselves to ensure that control of the town would continue to be in the hands of a council having one religious and political colour. Their regular income was derived from tolls collected at the fairs and markets, from rents of properties belonging to them, from services provided at the times of the races, and from capital sums provided by the members of the Council themselves and others concerned with the management of the town's affairs, its amenities and prosperity. Most improvements were financed by public subscription. The Council employed a chamberlain, who was both treasurer and town clerk, but who acted under the Steward appointed by the lords of the manor. We are fortunate that the chamberlains' accounts from 1564 are among the records now in the County Record Office in Dorchester, having survived the 1731 fire. They contain a great deal of information concerning the borough's affairs, and record payments made for the relief of the poor, the maintenance of the grammar school and for the erection in 1593, at a cost of £197 12 2, of a new guild hall. They record that some stone from the old hall was used and that additional stone was fetched from Pentridge.

The responsibility for the care of the poor of the town was, by the Elizabethan poor law of 1601, transferred to the parish, which was by this time responsible for the more essential functions of local government. The town of Blandford had grown very much larger than the borough, and there were difficulties of administration as parts of it were in the parishes of Bryanston, Blandford Forum, Blandford St Mary, Pimperne and Langton Long Blandford. It seems that these were overcome and that no-one in the town was left uncared for.

The manor of Bryanston came into the hands of the Rogers family early in the 15th century. The earliest noted is John Fitz Roger, who was married to Elizabeth, daughter of Sir Symon de Ferneaux. In his Will John Fitz Roger expressed the wish to be buried at St Martins Church, Bryanston. Richard Symonds' diary of 1644 contains many details of the memorials and interior of old Blandford Church as it was in the Civil War period, and records a marble tomb with the inscription: 'Here lyeth buried Sir John Rogers of Branston, Knight, Steward of this town of Blandford, who married Katrine, the daughter of Sir Richard Weston, Knight, and had be her sixteen sons and four daughters, which Sir John Rogers died the 22nd day of July at Beket in Berkshire at the house of my Lady Essex, and from thence brought to this towne of Blandford and buried under this tomb 16 of August 1565.'

The family vault below the east end of the nave of Blandford Forum Parish Church collapsed a few years ago, revealing coffins containing pre-1731 burials of members of the Rogers family.

One of his sons, Sir Richard Rogers (1527-1604), was a most remarkable man, who managed to attain high positions under the Crown in the county and town but, at the same time, was able to involve himself in the disposal of goods brought by sea to West Lulworth and elsewhere by pirates and smugglers. It would seem that quite a few Dorset gentlemen, including Sir Walter Raleigh of Sherborne, were similarly engaged. Sir Richard became High Sheriff of Dorset in 1573/4 and many of his activities were overlooked due to his loyalty to the Queen, his ability to raise money, men and arms in her service, and his general reputation as a kindly, good-natured man, who could always be relied upon for help in times of need.

The Ryves family were first noted in Blandford about 1535. They purchased Damory Court in 1549 and were also generous to the people of the town. The first known resident was Robert Ryves (1490-1551). Several of his descendants achieved considerable success in life. George Ryves was warden of New College Oxford in 1599; Thomas Ryves was a master in chancery in 1618 and a judge of the Faculty and Prerogative Court in Ireland. Bruno Ryves became chaplain to Charles I in 1628.

Queen Elizabeth died on 24 March 1603, the last of the Tudors, and so ended an era of great national achievement and the old order in Blandford.

Appendix 1

THE BLANDFORD FORUM MUSTER ROLL OF 1542

Key: A=Archer, AA=trained, B=Billman, G=Gunner.
'Harness' indicates possession of a suit of armour.

A	Jn Jonys	harness for man bow ½sh.arr
AA	Hen Breme	servant
A	Jn Adowne	
AA	Walt Colyns	
AB	Jn Maynard	
	Rob Ryve	2 pr harness for man bill bow sh.arr 2 swords 2 daggers horse
AB	Jn Pynge	2 harness for man 2 bills bow sh.arr horse
	Nic Gardyner	harness for man 2 bills bow sh.arr horse
AB	Tho Feffer	servant
A	Hen Romsey	
A	Jas Tylly	
A	Jn Caffe	harness for man sh.arr horse
AB	Wm Pytte	harness for man bill horse
	Pet Monsell	harness for man bow sh.arr
AB	Edw Pytt	coat of fence splints bill bow sh.arr
	Hen Wynter	sallet pr splints bill bow ½sh.arr
	Wm Godard	coat of fence sallet splints bill
	Jn Clement	2 bills
	Tho Rawlynson	harness for man
AA	Jn Ster	servant
A	Ant Aisshwood	
AA	Tho Crostelow	sword dagger
AA	Aukert Mathew	bow sh.arr
AB	Tho Bremley	dagger
	Jn Olyver	bow sh.arr sword dagger
AA	Jn Parker	servant bow
AA	Phil Goddard	bow ½sh.arr sword dagger
	Hen Poldon	bill
	Wm Vye	bow ½sh.arr
AA	Jn Shephard	servant
AB	Hugh Arnoll	
	Rob Hoper	sallet bill
AB	Rob Hall	bill
AB	Jn Johens	bill
	Jn Clerke	bow ½sh.arr
	Jas Bigges	bill dagger
	Jn Senyor	bow ½sh.arr
AB	Wm Jonge	bill
	Jas Peers	bill
	Ric Sprynge	bill
	Rob Bryckett	dagger
	Jn Loder	bill
AB	Tho Gurdeler	bill
	Walt Harris Ric Morant	2 bills
	Walt Lamberd	bill

AB	Tho Throsbowe	bill ½sh.arr
	Tho Jenkyns	bow sword dagger
	Hen Moskyll	dagger
AB	Edw Davye	bill
	Robt Sondyll Jn Asshewod	2 bills
	Wm Aissehopole	bow sh.arr
	Ric Hunte	sword
	Wm Jenkyns	coat of fence sallet bill
	Tho Scutt	bill bow ½sh.arr
	Jn Godard	bill bow sh.arr sword dagger
A	Rob Call	2 bills bow ½sh.arr
AB	Ric Harris	
	Jas Byson Fran Bylott	2 bills
	Jn Fylde	bill
	Wm Fyssher	sword
AA	Rob Stokys	bow
AA	Wm Pevye	bow
A	Jn Border	
	Nic James	bill bow sh.arr
	Edm Lamberd	glaive gun
	Pet Param	bow sh.arr
	Elwey Bygod	bill sword dagger
AG	Lamberd Harris	Ducheman
AG	Guyllam Carbone	
	Hen Corsom	Frenchman bill
G	Gerott Janson	
AB	Jn Waryn	
AB	Jn Wolff	bill
AB	Davy Coteler	sword dagger
AA	Jn Haukyns	
A	Rob Logge	
A	Tho Frankelyn	
	Rob Penne	
A	Rob Pelly	
AA	Jn Ryvys *(at)*	Damerecort harness for 2 men horse
	Rob Bastard	harness for man
	Hen Domber	bill
	Jn Pache	bill
A	Wm Haverlay	
A	Geof Bull	
AA	Alan Browne	
AB	Tho Wyggyns	
AB	Sim Taylor	
AA	Tho Hyll	
AB	Edw Cortenay	
AB	Rob Hookey	

Appendix II
THE BLANDFORD SUBSIDY ROLL OF 1525

The following residents were liable to taxes at this time:
1525 Blandforde Burgus

James Perys
Peter Parham
Stephen Sheyrey
John Maynard
Richard (   )
Robert Bastard
John Bemond
Mathew Battkyn
John Tanner
Joan Eyre wid
John Potell
John Fyscher
John Browce
Thomas Dawys
William Knyght
Harry Wenter
Robert Bulgyn
John Whytte
Peter Garatt
John Dackham
Katherine Howles wid
Nicholas Gardyner
Robert Gardyner
Robert Hooper
Harry Page
Total *(£18.12.10)*

Richard Dumber
Richard Arnold
John Pyng
Rawlyn Pyard
Robert Ryve
Nicholas Hewett
John Hewett
John Kyng
William Kyng
Thomas Sherly
Richard Devett
John Acovyntre
Peter his servant
Andrew his servant
Thomas Golde
Robert Cowper
William Wolffe
William Ludlow
Thomas Long
John Benett
Robert Vele
Edward Norton
Edward Langeford
Ancrette Mathew
William Churcheheye

John Pytte
William Pytte
William Browne
Richard Byrde
John Fawkener
John Robynson
Edmond Sawter
Joan Hayne wid
Richard Shephurde
Isaac Mychell
Thomas Benett
Thomas Weffet
Edmond Brach
John Mawncell
John Harvyst
Sampson Daschwood
Richard Sprynge
Nicholas Nowell
Robert Hownett
(or Holbonett)
Robert Whyttlocke
William Clarke
Walter Vere
Thomas Skette

THE WARNERSHIP OF PIMPERNE tithing in Blandford Forum

1525 The Waryn of Blanford

John Ye . . . .
William Vyne
John . . . .
John Collys
Gyllam Frencheman
Total *(£3.10.10)*

John D . . . .
John F . . . .
William Hall
Walter Carpenter
Robert Coke

Thomas Mychell
William Bayly
Mawde Smerte?
William Whyte
Richard Page

OPPOSITE: Bronze-age cinerary urns from Pond Barrow at Gussage St Michael, c1500 BC; (DCM) ABOVE: Iron-age fort on Hod Hill showing later Roman military camp. (BM)

Brictel ten' de .co. LITELTONE. Ulueue tenuit T.R.E. 7 geld'
p. v. hid. Tra. e. iii. car. In dnio. e una car. 7 vi. bord. 7 ii. servi.
Ibi molin redd' vii. sol. 7 vi. den'. 7 xx. ac' pti. 7 xxx. ac' pasture.
Valuit. iiii. lib. modo. xl. solid.
Brictel ten' de .co. BLENEFORD. Aluuard tenuit T.R.E. 7 geld' p. i.
hida 7 dimid'. Tra. e. i. car. Redd. xii. sol. Valuit xx. solid.
Robt' ten' de .co. WINTREBURNE. Goduin tenuit T.R.E. 7 geld'
p. ii. hid. Tra. e. i. car. q ibi. e cu. iii. bord. 7 iii. qx pasture. Valet
Robt' ten' de .co. WINTREBURNE. Aluuard xx. solid
tenuit T.R.E. 7 geld' p. iii. hid. Tra e. ii. car. Ibi st. vii. coscez
cu dimid car. 7 ii. qx silue. 7 pastura. iii. qx lg. 7 una qx lat. Valet
Ipse. Eps. ten' WINBURNE. de .co. Aschil tenuit T.R.E. xx. solid.
7 geld' p. iii. hid. Tra. e. ii. car. In dnio. e una car cu. i. servo. 7 v.
bord. Ibi molin redd' ii. sol. 7 ii. ac' pti 7 dim'. Pastura. v. leu
lg. 7 iiii. qx lat. Silua. vi. qx lg. 7 ii. qx lat. Valuit

OPPOSITE ABOVE: Busbury Rings Iron age camp, two miles from Blandford on Wimborne Road; (BM) LEFT: early British urn from Racecourse Down c150 BC; (DCM) CENTRE: Roman spearhead from near Tarrant Abbey, (BM) RIGHT: Small storage jar from Fontmell Parva. New Forest ware c250 AD. (BM) ABOVE: mosaic pavement at Hinton St Mary, showing head of Christ and the chi-ro symbol of Christianity; (DCM) BELOW: extract from Domesday Survey of 1085/6 showing Blandford entry. (DRO)

Blanforde Forum.

An Entrie of the Tenantes within the said Burrough who claime their Burgages by grant from her Matie, as Freeholders.

Thomas Godderd gent for one Burgage, garden and backsyde adioyninge yeldinge per annum — vij d

Richarde Swayne for one Burgage beinge sometime 4 burgages with garden and backside adioyninge yeldinge per annum — viij d

Christofer Domadge for one Burgage with garden & backside yeldinge per annum — iij d ob

The heires of William Kinge for one burgage sometime two burgages with garden and backside yeldinge per annum — v d

Christofer Domadge for one Burgage with garden yeldinge per annum — iij d ob

Thomas Kinge for one Burgage with gardeninge yeldinge per annum — vj d ob

The same Thomas one other Burgage & gardin yeldinge per annum — vj d

Richarde Chapman one burgage and gardine yeldinge per annum — vj d

Robert Herbert for one burgage sometimes iij burgages and garden yeldinge per annum — viij d

Thomas Godderd gent one burgage & gardin yeldinge per annum — v d

Christofer Domadge one burgage and gardin yeldinge per annum — vj d

The same Christofer one other Burgage yeldinge per annum — vj d

Richarde Rogers esquire one Burgage yeldinge per annum — v d

William Olyver one burgage yeldinge per annum — v d

John Bramble & Thomas Meddo in the right of their wyves, one burgage yeldinge per annum — v d

Christofer Domadge one burgage yeldinge per annum — v d

Edwarde Marshall one burgage yeldinge per annum — vj d

Thomas Godderd gent one burgage yeldinge per annum — v d

The heires of Roger Newburrowgh esquire one burgage yeldinge per annum — v d

[illegible]

Schedule of Duchy of Lancaster burgage tenants showing rents payable, 1591. (BM)

ABOVE: Interior of Rogers family vault under Blandford Forum parish church; (SJ) LEFT: plate from coffin of Sir Richard Rogers' daughter in Blandford Forum parish church, (SJ) and RIGHT: Rev Dr Bruno Ryves, chaplain to Charles I and II. (BM)

Fontevrault Abbey. (BM)

Dame Marie's Manor

The area of Blandford east and north of Damory street was held in the early 13th century as part of the Honour of Leicester by Robert, Earl of Leicester, from King John, whose favourite hunting ground, Cranborne Chase, extended to Blandford.

Following the Norman conquest, vast areas of western France came into common ownership with England under the English Crown, and we were as one country separated by the English channel. In this situation it was not uncommon for French religious orders to found monasteries for monks or nuns in England, either by taking over existing establishments or by creating new ones. One such order was that of Ste Marie, which had its mother church at Fontevrault near Saumur in the Loire valley of France – it is still there. Always favoured by the Counts of Anjou, Fontevrault acquired a tremendous reputation, particularly when the Counts became Kings of England. Members of the most aristocratic families joined the order and no fewer than fourteen of the nuns who rose to become its abbesses were princesses of the blood Royal. One of their houses in England was the Abbey of Amesbury in Wiltshire, and it was here that Queen Eleanor of Provence, the widow of Henry III, died in 1292 and where, later, Mary the daughter of Edward I, was admitted as a nun.

Earl Robert, on arranging for one of his daughters to enter the nunnery at Amesbury in about the year 1200 decided, with the consent of King John, to release some of his land at Blandford to the Order of Ste Marie, who would thereafter receive the rents. The rental was stated to be ten marks per annum (a mark was two thirds of one pound). In giving this consent the King was no doubt influenced by the fact that his father, Henry II (d 1189) and his brother Richard I (Coeur de Lion d 1199) were buried in the church at Fontevrault. His Mother, Queen Eleanor of Aquitane, was later buried there in 1204.

Thus the senior abbess of the order became lord of this newly formed manor at Blandford and was free to deal with it as she pleased, subject to the consent of the Crown. King John last visited Blandford on 17 August, 1216 and died on 19 October of that year.

This manor was subsequently given a name by which it could be identified; it is referred to in a transaction which took place in 1363/

4, whereby one John de Bridemere was authorised by Edward II to hold part of the manor of 'Dame Marie place de Chepyingblaneford', and recited that the said John de Bridemere, who was rector of Langton Long Blandford, had acquired it from the abbess of Fontevrault ('de abbatissa Fontis Abraudi'). This related to the disposal of part only of the manor comprised in the original gift by the Earl of Leicester. By this time the Anglo-French pronunciation would have sounded very much as we pronounce Damory today, ie as though it had two 'm's' in the middle. This release by the abbess to John de Bridemere included the site of St Leonard's Chapel, which the order of Ste Marie, Fontevrault had originally erected in the early 13th century as a hospital for the care of the sick of the town, and for use by travellers returning from the crusades. Some of the architectural features can still be seen, but these are of a subsequent rebuilding of the chapel in later mediaeval times. The last time the chapel was used appears to have been on 13 September 1760, when the Vicar of Blandford christened triplets Ann, John and James Bastick there. They were the children of Samuel Bastick, huntsman to Sir William Codrington of Langton.

By 1444 England had lost most of its territories in France and many of the French religious orders with abbeys in England were obliged to vacate them and to surrender their lands and possessions to the English Crown. By this time the income from the manor was being paid to another house of the Order at Grovebury by Leighton Buzzard. On this priory being deprived, the manor of Dame Marie at Blandford passed to William de la Pole, Marquess of Suffolk and Alice his wife, who in 1446 assigned it, with the consent of the King, for the benefit of the newly founded college of Eton by Windsor. Eton College did not have the benefit of the income for long as the manor was subsequently regranted to John Duke of Suffolk and Elizabeth his wife. In 1481 Edward IV authorised 'our beloved cousin John Duke of Suffolk and Elizabeth his wife, our best beloved sister' to assign the manor of Dame Marie at Blandford to 'the royal and collegiate chapel within the castle of Windsor, founded in honour of the Virgin Mary, St George and St Edward King and Confessor'. This was, of course, the present St George's Chapel.

The Eton college archives contain numerous leases of the manor to various tenants and, throughout the period in which they received the income, the manor was called 'Damariscourt'. The archives at Windsor Castle also contain leases to various tenants at Blandford, and in these the manor is variously described as Damariscourt by Blandford (1481), Damerycourte next Blandford (1499), and Damarycourt (1507).

By deed of grant of 20 December 1546, now preserved in the Windsor archives, the Clerk, Dean and Canons of Windsor gave to King Henry VIII 'the manor of Damarycourte in the County of

Dorset with appurtenances . . .' This was, in fact, in exchange for several rectories in Devon.

Soon after the death of Henry VIII in 1547, his son, Edward VI, granted 'the manor, farm, messuage and land in Blandford Forum, Langton, Pimperne, Stourpayne and Nutford' to the Duke of Somerset, who had already been granted the site of the abbey at Amesbury by Henry VIII on the dissolution of the monasteries. The Duke of Somerset disposed of his manorial rights in Blandford by assigning them in 1549 to Robert Reve. This Robert Reve, who was the same person as Robert Rives or Ryves, had purchased the Ranston estate in Shroton in 1545. He was born in 1490 and died in 1551, when he was described as being 'of Damory Court'. He was the earliest known progenitor of the English branch of the family of Ryves (probably pronounced Reeves) who held estates in various parts of Dorset and elsewhere.

It is possible that the first principal residence, known as Damory Court, was built before he purchased the estate outright and that he had occupied it as tenant. He is shown in the Blandford muster roll of 1542, which was a schedule of various people who could provide arms etc, in the event of war, as being of Blandford, and able to provide two suits of armour, a bill, a bow, a sheaf of arrows, two swords, two daggers and a horse. He was obviously the principal resident.

The famous divine, Dr Bruno Ryves, was born at Damory Court in 1596. He became chaplain to Charles I in 1628, Dean of Windsor in 1660 and secretary to the Order of the Garter. He died in 1677 and is buried in the south aisle of St George's Chapel, Windsor.

The Ryves family did not live at Damory Court for many years, as they were known to have favoured the greater seclusion of their other residence at nearby Ranston. The greyhound cresting the Ryves coat of arms is identical to that used by the famous firm of artists' colour merchants of Reeves, who confirm that the firm's founders descended from the Blandford and Ranston branches of the Ryves family. The greyhound also appears on the Greyhound Inn at Blandford. The inmates of the Ryves almshouses in Salisbury Street, founded by George Ryves in 1682, were always required to wear a badge depicting a greyhound on their outer garments.

The main residence was vacant for a while during the Civil War period, as it was made available for occupation by Lady Mary Bankes after her ejection from Corfe Castle in 1646. Lady Mary, who so resolutely defended the castle against the parliamentary forces, came to live at Damory Court while Kingston Lacy house was built. She died at Damory Court on 11 April 1661 before Kingston Lacy was finished. She was buried in old Blandford church. Although she was known as 'brave Dame Mary', the claim that Damory Court was named after her cannot be correct.

Frequent references to the property appear in the 17th, 18th and 19th centuries in rating assessments and other documents, and it is described variously as Damarie, Damery, Damory Court and as Damory Farm, Damory House and Damory Place.

Hutchins tells us that a little north of the house was a remarkable oak tree which became known as the Damory Oak. In 1747 it measured 75 feet high, the branches extended 72 feet, the trunk was 12 feet in diameter at 17 feet above the ground and the circumference on the surface of the ground was 23 feet. There was a cavity at the bottom 15 feet wide and 17 feet high which would hold 'near twenty men'. It is said that during the Civil War, and until after the Restoration, an old man sold ale in it. It was sold standing for £14 0 0 in 1755 and rooted up for firewood. No doubt the present Oakfield Street is a clue to the former means of access to the tree.

In 1774, Damory Court Farm was offered for sale 'with a good stone built farmhouse covered with stone tile, a large brick and tiled barn with granary, stables and other convenient outhouses and 133 acres of arable meadow and pasture'. It is clear from this that what was being offered for sale was something less than the original manor of Dame Marie of mediaeval times, the extent of which in its hey-day has not yet been precisely determined but included the eastern part of Blandford Forum, the greater part of West Pimperne, Damory Down, The Milldown, Nutford and parts of Stourpaine and Langton. The purchaser was Francis Kingston of Blandford, who developed the holding into a prosperous nursery and seed-growing establishment. It eventually passed to John Kingston Galpine, who continued the nursery and was in a substantial way of business. A rare catalogue of his was recently discovered and has been identified as the oldest of its kind known to have been issued in England and to have survived. It tells us what the gardeners of Georgian England were buying to plant in their gardens in 1782. (It has recently been re-produced with added commentaries and is available in local bookshops under the title *The Georgian Garden.*)

W. G. Maton, writing in 1797, refers to Damory Court as then partly modernised and that the Royal arms could still be seen over the doorway. The property subsequently passed to Lord Ashburton who appears as owner of this, and considerable other property in Blandford, in the 1837 tithe apportionment map. He later sold it to Christopher Good of Tarrant Hinton, from whom it descended to the present owners. The house was burnt to the ground on 7 March 1845.

The break-up of the Blandford part of the estate came at about this time, when the area was developed for housing purposes, to become known as New Town. The railway station and yards were in the general area of the main residence.

It has many times been written by historians that Damory Court was so named because Roger d'Amorie, who had been created a baron by Edward II and was Constable of Corfe Castle, had lived here and given his name to the place. While it is true that Roger d'Amorie held extensive estates in Dorset under the King, and was allowed to enclose large areas of Cranborne Chase, and did hold land as near to Blandford as Stubhampton, there is no evidence of his residence at Blandford or of his giving his name to this manor which I believe was so named by the Abbess of Ste Marie, Fontevrault on it being assigned to her in or about the year 1200.

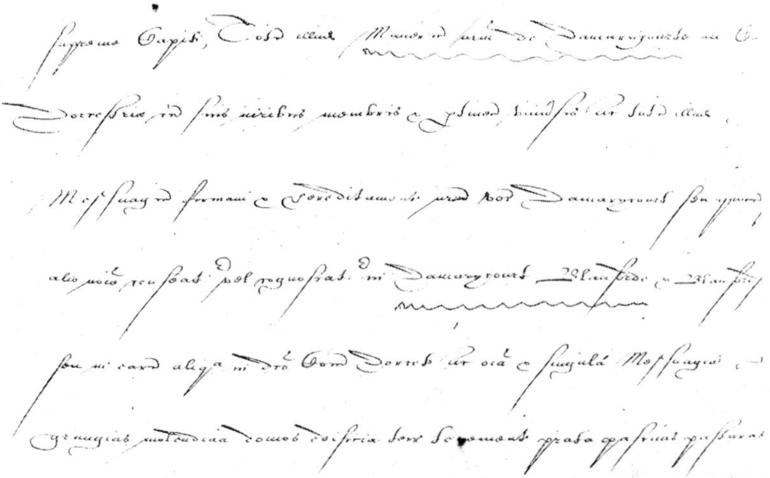

ABOVE: Extract from deed of gift of the manor of 'Damarycourte' to Henry VIII, 20 December 1546, (BM) and BELOW: remains of St Leonard's chapel from the north. (BM)

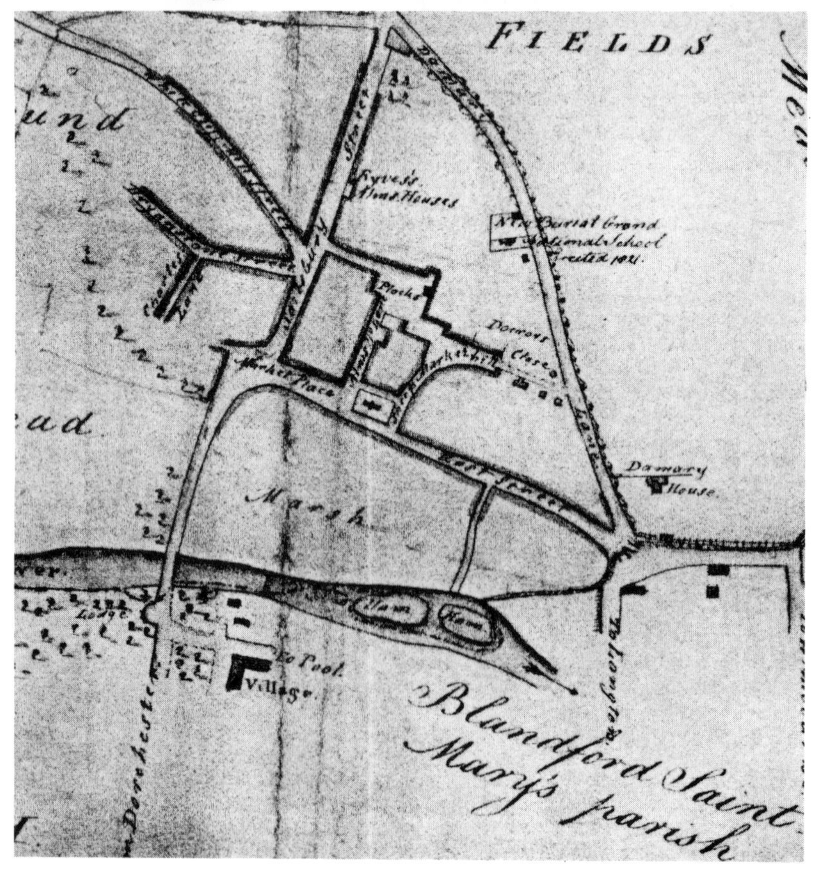
FIELDS
Damory
House
Village
Blandford Saint
Mary's parish

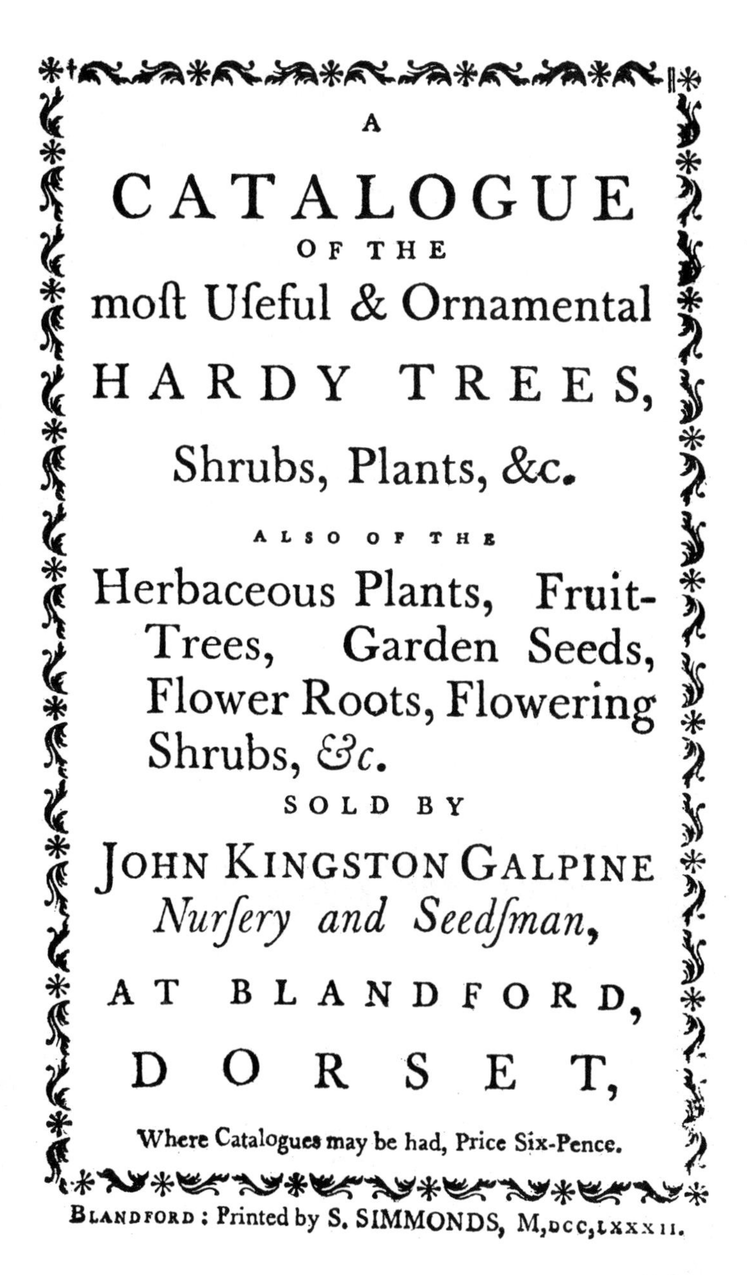
A
CATALOGUE
OF THE
most Useful & Ornamental
HARDY TREES,
Shrubs, Plants, &c.
ALSO OF THE
Herbaceous Plants, Fruit-Trees, Garden Seeds, Flower Roots, Flowering Shrubs, &c.
SOLD BY
JOHN KINGSTON GALPINE
Nursery and Seedsman,
AT BLANDFORD,
DORSET,
Where Catalogues may be had, Price Six-Pence.

BLANDFORD: Printed by S. SIMMONDS, M,DCC,LXXXII.

OPPOSITE LEFT: Arms of the Ryves family of Blandford and Ranston; (BM) RIGHT: the Damory Oak, (BM) and BELOW: detail of 1822 survey showing the position of Damory House. (DRO) ABOVE: Title page of J.K. Galpine's catalogue of 1782. (BM)

From Philip Lea's map of Dorset 1690.

Chartered Borough

Soon after he came to the throne in 1603, James I set about the task of bringing some uniformity into local government by imposing responsibilities upon unchartered boroughs calculated to benefit the public at large. Blandford Borough was in need of some clarification of its rights and customs, which had been acquired haphazardly over several centuries without any legal authority. The town was therefore given a charter of incorporation on 15 November 1605, a few days after the unsuccessful attempt by Guy Fawkes and his followers to blow up the Houses of Parliament. The grant was stated to be 'on the humble petition of our beloved subjects the now bailiff and inhabitants of Blandford'. It confirmed most of the town's privileges and customs and recited that it would result in 'the better government, rule and bettering of the said borough'. At the same time he granted the lordship of the manor to the Borough, subject to an annual fee farm rent of £8 3 7¾d. The Borough continued to pay this to the Duchy of Lancaster until the Duchy sold off the right to the rents to The Society of Merchant Venturers in 1708. Payment continued to be paid by the Borough Council to them until shortly before local government reorganisation in 1974, when the liability was extinguished on payment of a lump sum.

The charter did not confer upon the Borough the right to have its own magistracy, nor the right to send members to Parliament, and it did not extend the boundaries to include the whole town and parish. These were major disappointments to the town leaders, and one wonders if the charter was imposed rather than pleaded for as stated in the document. It confirmed Edward Machem in his office of bailiff and chief citizen and named the capital burgesses and councillors as Edward Machem, John Rawlinson, Robert Keynel, John Cleaves, Christopher Cornage, John Pitt, Jonadab Sherley, John Gawler, George Harbin, Robert Swaine and Thomas Pitt. They held office for life and could only be removed for gross misconduct.

There is no evidence that the granting of the charter had any marked effect on life in Blandford and this must be because, for these times, its affairs had been reasonably well conducted before the grant. The Council's prime function under the new order was much as it had been before, ie the maintenance of the commercial importance of the town, its markets and fairs in particular. Its entire income in 1623, in addition to any profit made at the time of the races, was:

	£	s	d
Tolls of the markets and fairs	44	0	0
Rent from the Marsh	4	0	0
Use of the hurdle house		10	0
Rent of the out-hays		13	4
Rent of the bowling green	1	6	8

The Borough looked forward to the Blandford race meetings and the following account shows the profit made in 1603 by John Cleves, the town steward, who organised the event:

Money received at the Races					
On Sunday, Supper				17	6
Monday, Dinner			2	14	6
ditto Supper			9	6	6
Tuesday, Dinner			7	15	6
ditto Supper			10	7	6
Wednesday, Dinner			10	6	11
ditto Supper			9	6	5
Thursday, Dinner and Supper			16	9	3
Friday, Dinner and Supper			11	10	6
Saturday, Dinner			4	1	8
			82	16	3
Received by the Play, six nights			11	7	1
Received for what was left:					
Bread and beef	11	6			
Fish and candles	4	6			
Suit and Dripping	10	0	1	6	0
			95	9	4
The sum total disbursed on this account			69	6	0
Profit on ditto			26	3	4

The Civil War and subsequent Commonwealth of the mid-17th century resulted in considerable hardships to those living in Blandford. The leaders of the town, who had declared for the King, were concerned to keep the river crossing and local highways free at all times for the use of the Royalist troops. Blandford was never garrisoned on a permanent basis, and it was with comparative ease that the Parliamentary troops under Sir William Waller were able to enter it in 1643. On this occasion he imposed a fine of £500 on the inhabitants, presumably for being on the side of the King. In 1644 the Parliamentary forces were again able to march in under the Earl of Essex, but they did not stay long, for the town was retaken by the King's forces, who held it until it was again taken for

Parliament under Major Sydenham. This was the story throughout 1644, and the poor people of Blandford were never quite sure which army they would have to find billets for from one day to the next. Major Sydenham's troops were allowed to plunder the town as a reprisal for capturing one of his messengers, but there is no evidence that they did any serious damage to property or that there was any loss of life. It was more a search for arms and ammunition, food and other comforts. Many accounts of the Civil War in Dorset state that on this occasion the High Sheriff of Blandford was hanged but this seems to be a misinterpretation of such records as there are. What did happen was that Captain George Starr, MP for Shaftesbury, and the other Parliamentary commanders seized the bailiff, Augustine Drake, and local commanders, and no doubt *threatened* to hang them but did not in fact do so. On 13 October 1644, during a lull in these troubles, Charles I was staying with his court at Bryanston, and attended church at Blandford where he read a lesson.

During the summer of 1645 local tradesmen, merchants farmers and landowners in Dorset had become so fed up with the continual disruption of their lives by the general unrest and the comings and goings of the opposing armies, that they banded together to protest and to protect their properties. They armed themselves with clubs and any other weapons they could find. These 'clubmen', as they were called, claimed to be neutral and held several demonstrations in various parts of the county, including at Badbury Rings and finally on Hambledon Hill, when nearly 2,000 of them were confronted by Cromwell's troops and persuaded to disperse, after some casualties had been inflicted on either side and some of the ring-leaders taken prisoner. One of these was Captain Richard Craddock, described as 'the malignant merchant of Blandford'.

In 1641 all males over the age of 18 were required to give an undertaking to support the rights of Parliament. The list for Blandford contains a certificate by the minister, churchwardens and overseers to the effect that 'none in this parish hath refused to take the protestation'.

During the Commonwealth period, Justices of the Peace, under the authority of Parliament, solemnised marriages in Blandford market and had the banns called there. The Bellman (town crier) had to announce the marriage on three succeeding Saturdays in the open market place. This extract from the Iwerne Courtney registers for 1655 refers to one such event:

'Thomas Crowten of Harrenden in the Parish of Iwerne Courtney in the County of Dorset, Husbandman, to Margaret Blandford of Melbury in ye County aoresaid spinster being both of ye age of XXI years and upwards having consented to live together in marriage were published three tymes in form followinge, that is to say in the open market at Sturminster Newton, upon the fourth daie of

October 1655 in the chappele at Harrenden aforesaid upon ye VII daie of the same October and in the open market at Blandford.'

Although the streets within Blandford Forum were much the same in the 17th century as they are now, so far as their general alignment and direction is concerned, the roads out of the town were, in some cases, taking different courses. John Ogilby's map of the district, published in 1675, shows the road to Dorchester turning left, after it had crossed Blandford bridge, towards Charlton Marshall, proceeding as far as the present village school at Blandford St Mary and then turning right in the direction of Dorchester. A map of Bryanston of about 1657/9 shows Bryanston street in Blandford as Chapel Lane. At that time it proceeded via Chapel Close across the park to a point north of the present church near the old Bryanston House. The river crossing was by a ford and footbridge. This road was closed in 1755 to exclude the general public from the deer park.

In the 1650s and 1660s the Borough and many of its traders issued copper or brass halfpenny and farthing tokens to facilitate trade, there being a shortage of coinage of small denomination, and they remained in circulation locally until made illegal by a Royal proclamation in 1672.

Charles II was proclaimed at Blandford in May 1660 and Walter Ridout, the Chamberlain, was paid £2 9 4d expenses.

Following this restoration of the monarchy, Blandford quickly reverted to its settled and peaceful way of life, with the parish and Borough officers sharing the duties of local government.

In 1685 Sir William Portman, a supporter of James II, was credited with being involved in the capture near Horton of the rebel Duke of Monmouth. Shortly after this, he purchased the Bryanston estate from the Rogers family.

In 1702 the Marquisate of Blandford was conferred upon John Churchill, the first Duke of Marlborough, the Churchills being then a prominent Dorset family.

Without any onerous functions, the Corporation of the 17th and 18th centuries, with a borough populaton of 1000 at the most, spent its income on small fees to minor officials such as the constable, macebearer, firemen, scavengers, pinder and others. They also accepted responsibility for the grammar school and the maintenance of the town hall. By far the biggest items of normal expenditure in any one year were on their own feasts, usually held at the Greyhound Inn, on the occasions of the Courts Leet, but also when anything could be found to celebrate. In addition to its own income, the Borough bailiff and capital burgesses were entrusted with the investment, management and control of capital moneys provided by numerous benefactors for the relief of the poor in the town, and in the almshouses and for education and other welfare work, the income being dispensed independently of the payments made under the poor law acts by the overseers of the poor appointed by the Vestry. The following decisions, extracted from the Borough minutes, indicate the sort of things they dealt with:

‘20.9.1773 Ordered John Penney to be arrested for his rent in arrear.

8.1.1734 Benjamin Barter should be Serjeant at Mace in the room of Robert Barter deceased.

2.12.1736 Mr Serjeant Hussey yr Steward of yr Burrough shall have two guineas at an yearly sallery whether he shall hold two Court Leets in one year or only one and his clerk 2 shillings and 6 pence.

27.7.1738 It would be convenient and proper that a woodhouse or woodhouses be erected for the use of the poor in the almshouse.

15.6.1739 John Beale to be Serjeant at Mace.

13.8.1739 Mr Ridout to be paid £20 and Mr Bastard £10 in part of their bills towards the town hall the total of whose bills are as under:

Mr Ridout's bill	£39	7	5
Mr Bastard's	20	8	0

and that the remainder shall be paid next year.

20.8.1739 Mr Bastard's estimate of £181 for rebuilding the church almshouses agreed.

1.4.1740 Wm Brookman, John Beale, Serjeants at Mace and Henry Jordan shall have a lease of the ffaire and markets for Ladyday last from the term of seven years at the yearly rent of £68.

24.6.1740 Bailiff to apply to Dean & Chapter of Winchester to know on what terms they will agree the lease to the Corporation of the great Tythes of this parish.

19.1.1741 All linnen which shall be hereafter given away at Christmas shall be of the manufacture of Great Britain or Ireland only.

23.11.1741 Agreed to distribute £30 out of Kingstons rent to the poor at Christmas there being £36 odd money now in hand and from four pounds secured to be paid at Christmas in full of farmer John Ware's rent to Michaelmas last.

20.12.1742 Scavengers Robert Pitman and Richard Dutton to be paid fifteen shillings per quarter to keep the market place, church street, east street and all other streets and squares within the Boro clean and the dung and filth removed weekly and to sweep weekly the passages to the church, town hall and the Cross and the pitching before the bailiff's door.

30.11.1743	It is ordered that the Serjeant shall have a new hatt yearly and gold lasse and buttons not exceeding the sum of Twenty shillings against Whitsunday.
9.12.1742	In future no tenants of houses belonging to the corporation to be roofed with reed or straw.
7.12.1752	Allowance for the bailiffs annual feast to be increased to £15.
16.5.1757	Robert Gutch (Reverend) appointed Master of school.
24.1.1764	Writ against William Lacy the pig dealer for taking a pig away after the same was in custody of Henry Beale the said pig having been seized for non payment of market toll to the borough.
1.10.1769	Bailiff and burgesses to be provided with superfine black cloth gowns faced with velvet and likewise the Serjeant at Mace is to have a blue cloth cloak trimmed with a broad gold lace down before and around the cope. It is likewise ordered that a mace be provided not to exceed the sum of £40 and that the gowns of such of the burgesses as may happen to die or resign shall be returned to the bailiff for the time being. Fine of ten shillings imposed for throwing rubbish into the streets.
2.11.1792	Two lamps to be placed at the town hall to be lit out of John Bastard's charity.
20.2.1798	Resolved that 100 guineas be subscribed for the defence of the Kingdom and the bailiffs allowance for his feast be discontinued during the war.
18.11.1800	Samuel Simmons ordered to remove bow windows projecting over the footpath.
27.9.1802	John Bastard appointed bailiff and Harry Biggs chamberlain.
3.7.1806	Council to pay 5 guineas towards proposed footway over the bridge, the County offered £40.
1.2.1812	Edmund Cooth, town clerk, resigned. Septimus Smith appointed in his place. Owner of Greyhound and others erecting porticos over the footpaths to pay acknowledgements to the corporation.
19.4.1820	Ordered that the pig market be removed to the sheep market.
13.5.1822	Cattle market moved to sheep market hill and tabernacle.
17.11.1823	Septimus Smith, Town Clerk, ordered to prosecute persons who let off fireworks on the 5th instant.
23.4.1824	Council agree to provide better accommodation for the quarter sessions in the town following complaints by magistrates.

In 1834 commissioners were appointed by Parliament to visit all the boroughs in the country to obtain information as to how they were being conducted, to report any illegal or undesirable practices, to investigate their finances and customs and to assess their future prospects and claims to retain their borough status. Edward J. Gambier who, incidentally, was counsel for the prosecution of the Tolpuddle Martyrs in 1834, was appointed to investigate Blandford Forum, including the parts not strictly in the Borough. He reported that the town had a bailiff, a steward, a town clerk, a chamberlain, two constables and a serjeant-at-mace, and that the bailiff was an ex-officio coroner and Justice of the Peace during his term of office and that the only court still being held in the borough was the Court Leet. He noted that there was no police force and that the town was not lit, and estimated that the future regular income of the Borough, without any special rates being levied, would be about £108 3 2d. The only matter upon which he reported unfavourably was the failure of the town to maintain proper law and order — these were his words:

'A great inconvenience is felt at Blandford from the unruly state of the population, from the want of a municipal authority, and from the defect of a constabulary force in that part of the town which is out of the borough. The population beyond the bounds of the borough is of a description which requires more control than that which is within, and there is only one constable or tythingman for all that part of the parish which is out of the borough. It is much desired by the corporation, and it seems to be for at least as regards the preservation of the peace and the preliminary enquiries into crimes and misdemeanours, should be confided to a body of civic magistrates.'

Following this report, Blandford Forum was created a municipal corporation, carrying the responsibilities imposed by the Municipal Corporatrions Act of 1835, but the Borough was not granted its own magistrates as recommended by Mr Gambier. It is somewhat surprising that it did not lose its borough status completely, as did many other boroughs at this time; possibly some considerable development, enlargement of the Borough boundaries and an increased population was envisaged, justifying retention of its status. The boundaries were eventually enlarged in 1889 and 1930.

The new Corporation, which had to be elected, was vested in a council of four aldermen and twelve councillors, from whom a Mayor was to be chosen annually and, for the first time, the people of Blandford, at least those who were entitled to a vote (and still a minority), could elect who they wished onto the council without regard to politics or religion. The new council was:

Mayor: Henry White
Aldermen: Henry White, John Dansey, Walter C. Heywood and Philip Abraham Barnes.

Councillors: John Durden (91) John Dansey Jr (89) John White (85) Henry Abbott (83) Joseph S. Daniell (82) Charles Cadie (70) Malachi Fisher (69) Simon Groves (68) John Shipp (65) Angel S. Hodges (59) William Pond (58) and Thomas H. Bennett (43).

(the figures in brackets are the votes cast for each)

The seargeant-at-mace was Samuel Kendall, the treasurer Percival North Bastard, the chamberlains William Pond and John Durden with Septimus Smith, town clerk.

In 1838 some efforts were made to enlist support in Blandford for the Chartist movement, but there was little enthusiasm. The *Dorset Chronicle* reported a meeting held at Charlton Down near Blandford as poorly attended and 'the number at any period could barely have exceeded 1500'. One of the Tolpuddle Martyrs, John Standfield, was there, and his uncle George Loveless, sent a message of support. This was the year of their return to England.

Thenceforth things settled down, the Borough Council conducting the affairs of the town to the best of its ability, raising special rates whenever any particular project required financing and generally complying with the Act of 1835. Some of their functions passed to the County Council on its formation in 1888, and so it continued until local government reorganisation in 1974 deprived the town of its borough status.

APPENDIX III

In 1641 all males over the age of 18 were required to sign an undertaking to support the rights of Parliament. The list for Blandford, reproduced below, should be a complete list of all such males in Blandford since no-one had refused. They did not actually sign as most of them were illiterate but their names were recorded.

Richard Higden
Stephen Biles
John Payne
John Lanninge
Robert Moore
Richard Harris
Robert Upward
Martein Cade
William Pooke
Robert Weston
George Ram
Thomas Foote
Edward Ellott
John Williams
William Lugges
William Gunter
John Weech
Thomas Jissoppe
Thomas Stronge
John Pitney
Thomas Wheler
William Keymer
Huighe Keymer
William Kemer
Christopher Keymer
William Wilkins
William Tatum
Anthony Lugges
George Elkins
Clement Tulke
John Turner
Thomas Barnes
Robert Cleeues
Nathaniell Galpen
Richard Sidlinge
Mathew Bernard
Nathaniell Clerke
Henry Potts
John Sprange
Ambrose Carpenter
Valentine Chappell
Christopher Parker
Robert Lighe
George West
Phillip Durrunt
Giles Smith
Robert Bizwell
Nicdholas Combe
Osmund Lufman
Nicholas Evans
Edward Browne
Thomas Harris
Arthure Lyle
Leonard Hennby
John Sampson
Richard Caddock
Matthew Page
Thomas Longe
Leonard Goold
John Merrett
Richard Sanford
William Gates
John Robinson
John French
David Thomas
Thomas Dey
Roger Ransome
Thamas Vature
Giles Warren
Huighe Blundell
Thomas Thorne
Thomas Baker
Thomas Cole
Sampson Potts
Richard Smith
Robert Kelway
William Newton
John Evans
Oliver Clerke
John Curtice
Edmond Scorie
Christopher Goold
John Arney
Edward Goold
Stephen Kent
John Dawe
John Combes
William Sheppard
Richard Mallord
Zorubbabel Maltus
William Vallett
William Higgens
Richard Deake (?)

Thomas Payne
Peter Harginge
Thomas Smithe
William Pitt
Penticost Spiney
Castell Cole
Samuel Palmer
John French
Jeremy Bizwell
Richard Sumers
Christopher Mitchell
Walter Elkins
Ro. Rogers
Matthew Bernard
Richard Harris
Christopher Bernard
Richard Horlocke
John Knight
John Bartlett
Thomas Goold
John Knight
John Shorthose
James Knight
Nicholas Pope
William Curtis
Nicholas Dier
Thomas Leggatt
Henry Moulton
Anthony Watts
Walter Sterle
Henry Knoker
William Whitmell
Robert Ridout
Alexander Arney
Christopher Studly
Jehonadab Sherley
Robert Harding
Augustine Drake
Richard Parker
Richard Corben
Thomas White
William Arney
Samuel Everard
William Cox
Robert Hayter
Richard Hulett
John Cottrell
Thomas Bizwell
Edmond Kinge
Richard Lighe
Walter Reynolls
Jesper Crosse
Henry Abbott
Peter Kinge
William Orchard
Phillip Gilbourne
John Evans
Robert Oliver
Robert Cox
William Joanes
George Clerke
Daniell Hamatt
William Oliver
Roger Freeman

Mathew Mitchell
Richard Cox
Robert Follatt
Clement Legrosse
Robert Newman
Nicholas Harbin
Robert Genge
Thomas Wotts
Christopher Launce
Christopher Haviland
Robert Harris
Nicholas Weech
William Savage
Roger Paule
John Okley
John Cutler
John Goudon
John Bisshop
Thomas Patch
Robert Baker
William Fuge
Richard Hoskins
Richard Shall
Roger Allen
Henry Diett
John Higgins
Nicholas Coward
Thomas Lane
William Devall
Zachary Togood
William Coward
Thomas Coward
William Allen
Thomas Bishop
John Miller
Thomas Drayton
Edward Atkins
Ezra Sh'erley
William Stretchly
John Hutchins
Richard Andrewes
Aldred Andrewes
Leonard Numby
John Oliver
Thomas Bishoppe
William Gawler
John Andrewes
Richard Welch
William Medens
Richard Woodman
Leonard Perry
John Gardner
Henry Lacie
William Hendy
Valerian Oline
Walter Ashe
Thomas Goolde
William Atkins
Henry Amye
Leonard Coffen
Owen Mellage
John Batt
Thomas Wotts
James Hilgroue

John Pounhall
John Muston
William Chepman
William Hurle
Richard Humby
Robert Wiat
John Davies
John Tresloe
John Kezer
Nicholas Robbins
Matthew Hardinge
Clement Perrye
John Launce
John Duffett
Nicholas Goold
John Scovile
Stephen Dibban
William Horlocke
William Sutton
John Major
John Guye
Andrew Brooke
Richard Goolde
William Gawler
Henry Pilconton (?)
Richard Clerke
Joseph Sneyden
Jeffry Phyander
John Francis
Robert Muñes
Richard Norman
John Gillett
Jonadab Gillett
John Evans
William Greene
Thomas Norman
Richard Rabbetts
Nathaniell Elmes
Thomas Stowell
Henry Flewell
John Mainard (?)
Richard Stayner
Thomas Levett
Simeon Pearce
Richard Drinkwater
Michaell Bastable
Joseph Rixon
William Dover
Edward Dier
John Veale
Thomas Godden
John Haysome
John Taler
Richard Stone
Richard Stone
Henry Payne
William Sherwood
Emanuell Anstie
John Tilley
William Arney
John Macham
Leonard Rabbetts
Thomas Dennish
Thomas Horlocke

Samuell Desmoulin
John Hasford
Thomas Pitt
John Harvey
John Fussell
George Bradford
Ambrose Vincent
John Sexton
William Wiatt
John Abbatt
Tho. Tregonwell, Esq.
Hubart Gaultan
Nicholas Furmage
Thomas Bolte
Edward Weeich
Ambrose Speed
Nicholas Lugges
Richard Hamlen
Thomas Dance (?)
Robert Dounton
Robert Weare
James Bolte
Robert Upwood
Thomas Batt
Nathaniell Gillett
William Arney
Richard Elkins (?)
Richard Pope
William Weare
John Easton
John Lyle
Robert Bayly
Henry Cane
Edward Weare
Robert Ashly
William Goldring
Raynold Speed
Peter Bennett
William Hamlen
Mathew Fry
Christopher Hulet
John Hart
William Parham
Robert Knighte
Simon Goddard
William Pinge
John Barnes
George Kezer
William Bizwell
Thomas Lee
William Horlocke
Henry Dackombe
None in this pishe hath refused to take the ptestation.
John Linsie, minister
Walter Ridout
William Frampton
churchwardens

Nathaniell Treslor
James Dares

overseers

Frauncis Chetle, Esq.
Mr John Chettle, senr
Mr John Chettle, jnr
Jaspar Humbey
Thomas Crosse
John Crosse
Willm. Dracke
Nich. Turner
Mathew Kaines
Simon Haukins
Richard Welch
John Haukins
Gregory Thourbourne
Mathew Compton
Christopher Symmes
Laurence Fiander
Richardd Bythewood
Andrew Lyde
John Vine
Willm. Webbe
George Haukinge

Appendix IV

A list of bailiffs from 1592 to 1834 and mayors from 1835 to 1860 will be found in the third edition of Hutchins' *History and Antiquities of Dorset.*

MAYORS FROM 1861

1861 Wm. C. Fincham
1862 Francis T. Johns
1863 Henry Durden
1864 Angell S. Hodges
1865 Wm. C. Fincham
1866 Joseph S. Daniell
1867 Francis T. Johns
1868 Spence Abbott
1869 Geo. W. Daniell
1870 Henry Gill
1871 Francis T. Johns
1872 Charles Pond
1873 Thos. H. Bennett
1874 Henry Durden
1875 Edward Fisher
1876 Spence Abbott
1877 Francis T. Johns
1878 Charles Pond
1879 Thos. E. Bennett
1880 Henry Durden
1881 Spence Abbott
1882 Henry Gill (ret.)
1882 Jax. Ball (part term)
1883 Robert Eyers
1884 Edgar B. Smith
1885 John W. Luff
1886 John W. Luff
1887 John W. Luff
1888 John W. Luff
1889 Philip A. Barnes
1890 Philip A. Barnes
1891 Philip A. Barnes
1892 Philip A. Barnes
1893 John Durden
1894 Charles H. Curtis
1895 Charles H. Curtis
1896 Edgar B. Smith
1897 James J. Ball
1936 Bertie C. Hunt
1898 Philip A. Barnes
1899 Philip A. Barnes
1900 Albert H. Hillyer
1901 Philip A. Barnes
1902 Alfred C. Woodhouse
1903 John I. Barnes
1904 John I. Barnes
1905 John I. Barnes
1906 John I. Barnes
1907 John I. Barnes
1908 John I. Barnes
1909 John I. Barnes
1910 John I. Barnes
1911 Edward Derham
1912 John J. Ball
1913 Sidney J. Norman
1914 Sidney J. Norman
1915 Joseph J. Lamperd
1916 Joseph J. Lamperd
1917 Joseph J. Lamperd
1918 Joseph J. Lamperd
1919 Louis B. Bunce
1920 Louis B. Bunce
1921 Alexander J. Hicks
1922 Alexander J. Hicks
1923 Alfred Hobbs
1924 Alfred Hobbs
1925 James Thomas Rankin
1926 Harold S. Woodhouse
1927 Harold S. Woodhouse
1928 Walter J. Newman
1929 Alexander J. Hicks
1930 Alexander J. Hicks
1931 Ellen G. Castleman-Smith
1932 Ellen G. Castleman-Smith
1933 Ellen G. Castleman-Smith
1934 Ellen G. Castleman-Smith
1935 Bertie C. Hunt
1937 Charles S. Tripp
1938 Charles S. Tripp
1939 John E. Conyers
1940 John E. Conyers
1941 Algernon J. E. Blandford
1942 Algernon J. E. Blandford
1943 Algernon J. E. Blandford
1944 Dennis S. Cuff
1945 Dennis S. Cuff
1946 Bertie C. Hunt
1947 Bertie C. Hunt
1948 Bertie C. Hunt
1949 Percy J. Lucas
1950 Ethel M. Biddulph
1951 Ethel M. Biddulph
1952 Charles B. Faulkner
1953 Ellen G. Castleman-Smith
1954 Joseph L. Carter
1955 Bertie C. Hunt
1956 John Trickett
1957 Richard J. W. King (died 7.10.57)
1957 George R. J. Hasket
1958 Agnes A. Williams
1959 Trevor W. Fowler
1960 Edward G. Riggs
1961 Joseph L. Carter
1962 Bertie C. Hunt
1963 Gwendolin F. Lane
1964 George R. J. Haskett
1965 Wilfrid L. Penny
1966 Agnes A. Williams
1967 Thomas L. Hughes
1968 Gordon Olaf Fry
1969 John Trickett
1970 Gwendolin F. Lane
1971 Arthur W. G. Adams
1972 Anthony N. Lane
1973 Albert Powis

Blandford Town Council
(Local Government Act 1972)

1974 Stanley E. Lawes
1975 Dr. David H. Davies
1976 Dr. David H. Davies
1977 Arthur W. G. Adams
1978 Gladys M. Cole
1979 Revd. Raymond O. Balmer
1980 Gwendolin F. Lane
1981 Dr. David H. Davies
1982 Revd. Raymond O. Balmer
1983 Gwendolin F. Lane

Honorary Freemen of the Borough

19 June 1918	Jack T. Counter, V.C.
17 April 1929	Lady Baden Powell
20 November 1935	Alderman Miss E. G. Castleman-Smith
14 June 1949	W. H. Wilson, Esq.
8 December 1953	W. J. Newman, Esq.
18 November 1955	The Dorsetshire Regiment
1 November 1956	Alderman Bertie C. Hunt
14 October 1970	Charles K. Lavington, Esq.
13 October 1972	The Royal Corps of Signals

The freedom granted to the Dorsetshire Regiment was extended in 1983 to the Devon & Dorset Regiment.
The above list does not include a large number of 'freedoms' granted to Blandford men who served in the Boer War (1899-1902).

LEFT: Arms of Borough of Blandford Forum; (BM) RIGHT: seal of Borough of Blandford Forum, (BM) and BELOW: Old Bryanston House and Chapel. House designed by James Wyatt, built 1778, demolished 1897. (SJ)

LEFT: Arms of Rogers of Bryanston; (BM) RIGHT: Sir William Waller, Parliamentary leader at Blandford, 1643, (BM) and BELOW: the Borough maces and loving cup. (SJ)

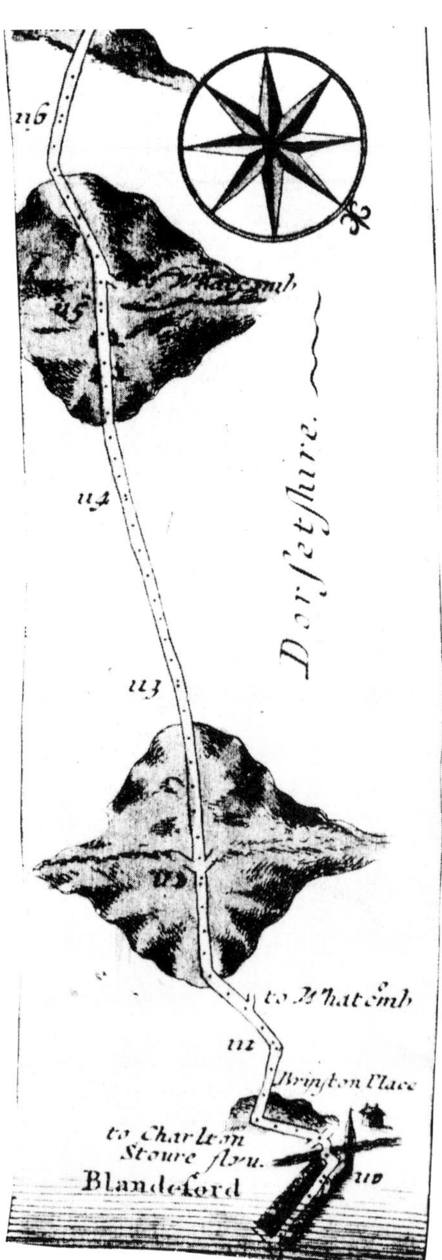

From John Ogilby's map of the road from London to Weymouth, 1675, and RIGHT: Mr J. G. Langridge, Blandford's present Town Crier. (S J)

1681 41

The account of Christopher Stoodly bailiffe for ye intrest of 50li given by Mr Kenal & others for clothing ye poor.

	~~0 3 0~~
Given Jon Downtom wife a change	0 – 3 – 0
Given wid Wares daughter a change	0 – 3 – 0
Given Margret Upward a change	0 – 3 – 0
Given Mary White a change	0 – 3 – 0
Given wid Sprage a change	0 – 3 – 0
Given wid Billis a change	0 – 3 – 0
Given Jeremes boy a shirt	0 – 2 – 0
Given Jon Liall a coat	0 – 7 – 8
Given Owen Mollage a coate cloth	0 – 7 – 8
Given Huets 2 boys 2 coats & one change	0 – 12 – 0
Given Bridget Apoll a change	0 – 3 – 0
Giv: Rogers his boy a shirt	0 – 2 – 0
Tho: Dory a shirt	0 – 3 – 0
Given wid Buttons boy a coat	0 – 5 – 0
	3 – 0 – 4

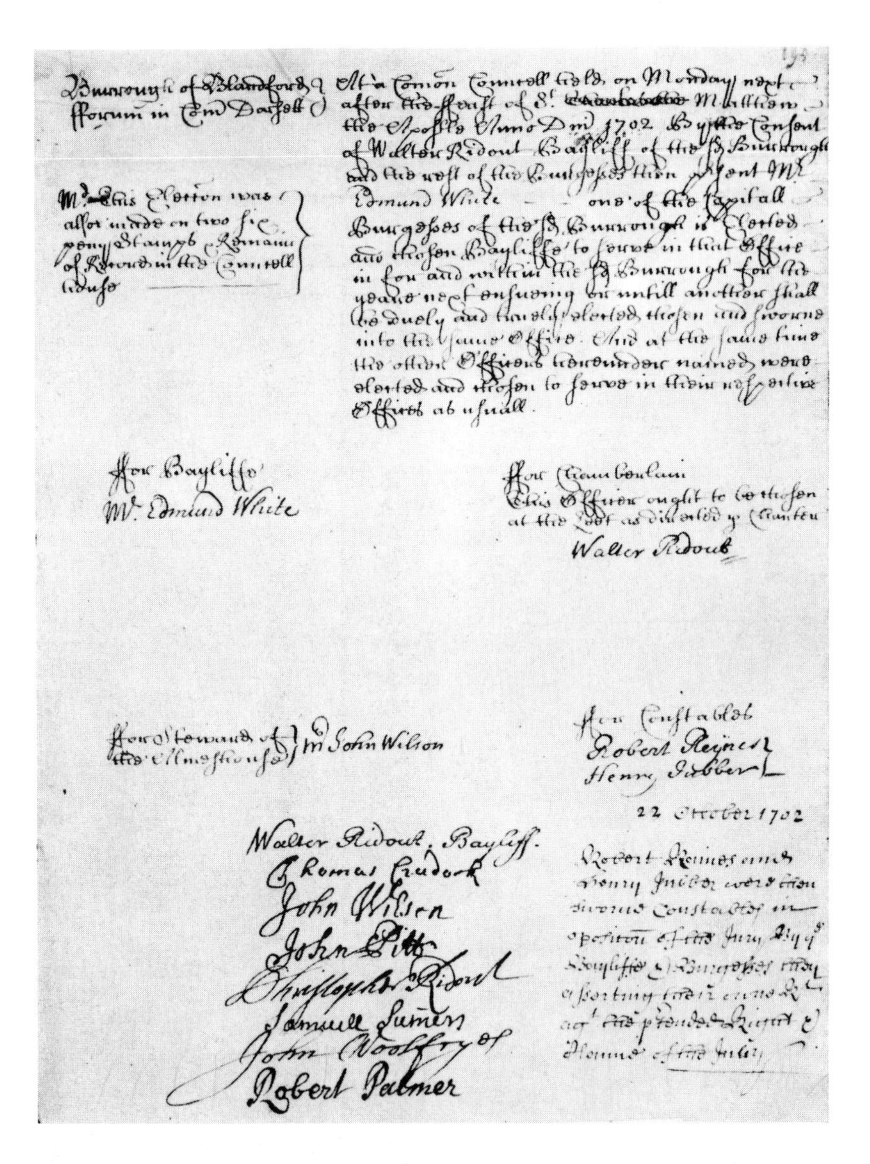

Burrough of Blandford fforum in Com Dorsett

At a Comon Councell held on Monday next after the ffeast of St. Michaell the Archangle Anno Dni 1702 By the Consent of Walter Ridout Bayliff of the sd Burrough and the rest of the Burgesses then present Mr Edmund White one of the Capitall Burgesses of the sd Burrough is Elected and chosen Bayliffe to serve in that Office in for and within the sd Burrough for the yeare next ensuing or untill another shall be duely and lawfully elected, chosen and sworne into the same Office. And at the same time the other Officers hereunder named were elected and chosen to serve in their respective Offices as usuall.

Mr [illegible] This Election was [illegible] on two [illegible] [illegible] of Record in the Councell house

ffor Bayliffe
Mr Edmund White

ffor Chamberlain
This Officer ought to be chosen at the Leet as directed by Charter
Walter Ridout

ffor Steward of the Almeshouse Mr John Wilson

ffor Constables
Robert Reynes
Henry Jubber

22 October 1702

Robert Reynes and Henry Jubber were then sworne Constables in opposition of the Jury [illegible] Bayliffe & Burgesses they asserting their right agt the pretended Right & Clayme of the Jury.

Walter Ridout, Bayliff.
Thomas [illegible]
John Wilson
John Pitt
Christopher Ridout
Samuell Sumers
John Woolfry
Robert Palmer

OPPOSITE ABOVE: Account of Christopher Stoodly, Bailiff of Blandford (1681) showing how he spent money given to the town for clothing the poor; (DRO) BELOW: old Post Office in West Street under flood about 1906, (JG) and ABOVE: appointment of Bailiff and other officers 1702; the appointments should have been made at the Court Leet. (DRO)

M

OPPOSITE ABOVE: The Borough Fire Brigade c1920; (BM) BELOW: Mayor's Day, 1956; Alderman Hunt, Mayor Trickett and Town Clerk, Charles Lavington. (BM) ABOVE: The Mayor and Corporation 1897, (BM) and BELOW: civic Procession led by Blue-coat boys, 1897. (JG)

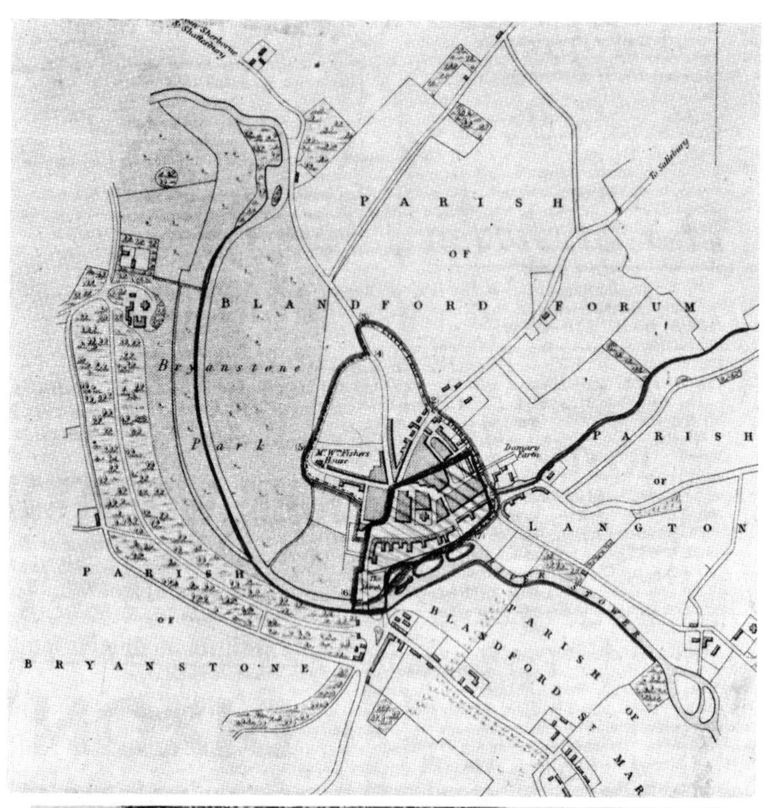

ABOVE: Plan taken from Blandford Boundary Commission Report 1837; the Borough is the hatched area, and BELOW: the Borough Council in 1912. (BM)

ABOVE: Mayor Edward Derham with Macebearers F. Goddard and T. Bartlett; (JG) BELOW: ceremonial opening of new Post Office in 1935. (BM)

We the undersigned request the favor of your calling a Public Meeting at Blandford, on such day as may be most convenient to take into consideration the propriety of forming a Plan for Watching the Town of Blandford *during the ensuing Winter.*

George W. I. Chard	*I. W. Smith*
Henry White	*E. B. Portman*
T. & W. Roe	*M. Fisher*
Henry W. Johns	*H. F. Fisher*
Stephen Carpenter	*R. Keynes*

John Dansey.

To the Bailiff of the Borough of Blandford.

Blandford, September 18*th*, 1829.

In compliance with the foregoing requisition I hereby appoint a Meeting to be held at the Guildhall on Thursday the 23rd of September Instant, at 11 o'Clock, for the above purpose.

J. White, Bailiff

Blandford, September 19*th*, 1829.

SHIPP, PRINTER, BLANDFORD.

There was no police force at this time. (DCM)

Law and Order

The century following the Norman conquest saw little change in the system of law enforcement in Dorset operative in late Anglo-Saxon times. Each area of the county was divided into a 'Hundred', Blandford being in Pimperne hundred, and each hundred contained a number of 'tythings' or groups of families. The head men of each tything were responsible for seeking out and punishing offenders and were subject to the overall authority of the Sheriff of Dorset. They held their own courts here and administered justice according to the custom of the day.

Gradually the authority of the county Sheriff was taken over by the local lord of the manor, to whom the King had granted the tenancy in chief. The lord's court at Blandford was called the Court Leet. Matters of great importance involving the conduct of the lord of the manor himself and serious offences against the King's peace were dealt with at the Dorset County Sheriff's own court.

The Blandford Forum Court Leet dealt with all minor crime, and infringements of manorial and local custom, changes of tenancy, and the duties to be performed by occupiers of the land under the lord of the manor. The lord was represented by a steward, who was usually a local lawyer. After 1399 the appointments of steward were made by the Duchy of Lancaster and, when the Borough received its charter of incorporation from James I in 1605, making it a free borough and exempt from any form of manorial control, it appointed its own stewards. At each Court Leet a jury was empanelled to hear the complaints brought against those summoned to attend. The first business at these courts was to appoint the town bailiff, the chamberlain, the constables and persons called 'assizors' whose job it was to ensure that the quality of ale, bread and other essentials were up to standard and to bring offenders to court, it being important that the markets and fairs of the town should have a good reputation in the eyes of persons coming to them, and also for the protection of the townspeople. The two constables were obliged to carry out the orders of the court and of the bailiff. Various other officers were appointed from time to time, such as the hayward, who looked after the common land and was responsible for the streets of the town; the rat catcher; the pinder, who locked up the stray animals and released them for a fee and the 'supervisors of the fires' who were firemen-cum-fire-prevention officers. The court also appointed the stewards of the almshouses and 'the searchers, sealers and regulators of leather'. The procedure continued with little change until the early 19th century.

The early records of the manorial court leet at Blandford are kept in the Public Record Office in London and date from the 14th century. The following are a few extracts from the court held on 7 October 1390, which bore the heading

'Court held on Wednesday on the morrow of St Faith the Virgin in the 14th year of the reign of King Richard the Second'.

'1. Alice Pulham (3d) wrongfully raised a hue and cry upon John Triewman, therefore she is in mercy.

2. The aletasters come. They present that Richard Bills (4d) once, Thomas Gogayne (8d) twice, John Triweman (4/3) twelve times, Henry Chynne (3/4) eleven times, John Curnuale (2-) six times, John Fletcher (2/4) seven times, John Deraunt (2/-) six times, John Drewe (20d) five times, John Helier (8d) twice, John Suyland (2/8) eight times Henry Sterk (4d) once, John Webbe (4d) twice, Alice Triweman (8d) twice brewed and broke the assize, therefore the same are in mercy.'

(the fines are shown in brackets).

The bakers were next before the court — probably for poor quality or short weight and the record reads:

'John Triewman (1d) Robert Huff (6d) John Hughes (2d) John Benet (2d) John Heller (3d) and Richard Ball (6d) bakers broke the assize of bread, therefore they are in mercy.'

Next on the list were the butchers, who were charged with buying and selling meat in the market on the same day, which was an offence. The entry reads: 'Richard Hert (2d) and John Laumel (2d) are common regrators of meat, therefore they are in mercy.'

From 1361 the criminal law in Blandford, as elsewhere, was administered by the Justices of the Peace acting under the county Sheriff, who was appointed by the King. Minor offenders were often conveyed by the constables to the home of a justice for summary trial. Serious offences were dealt with by the Justices of the County at various towns at quarterly meetings which became known as Quarter Sessions. The last of these to be held at Blandford was on 7 January 1825. All subsequent meetings were held at Dorchester instead of being held in turn at Dorchester, Blandford, Sherborne and Bridport. At Quarter Sessions the justices had a great deal to do, apart from trying criminals, as they were responsible for the making of regulations governing the administration of the county, its roads, bridges, prisons, the making of licensing laws, fixing wages for certain industries, prescribing standards of quality for bread and beer and, among other functions, deciding disputes arising under the poor laws. The justices sitting at Quarter Sessions in 1635, for example, dealt with such matters as the effect of a disastrous fire at Bere Regis, a dispute about gleaning rights at Sherborne, measures to prevent the spread of plague from Blandford and dangerous dogs at Beaminster. Other serious crime was dealt with by the King's Judges of Assize, who travelled from place to place on the western assize circuit. One of these, Sir Thomas Pengelly, died while at Blandford in 1730 from what was termed 'gaol distemper', which was prevalent among prisoners at that time. It was the custom for the Borough to wine and dine the judges and bishops and their staffs on the occasions when they held court at Blandford. The following items from the chamberlains' accounts are typical:

'1614	A bottle claret wine given the judges		1	4d
	One bottle of sack		2	0d
1625	Paid for a gallon of wine bestowed on Sir Warwick Heal		3	0d
1628	Paid for a shugar loaf 10¾lb, given Mr Swain (the Recorder)	1	1	6d
1629	Paid bailiff's expenses in spending a buck given to the town by Lord Suffolk	2	8	7d
1629	Paid for a gallon of wine presented to Judge Dennum (Sir John Denham)		4	0d
1631	Paid for gallon of wine given to the judges		3	8d
1631	Paid for wine and shugar 'Bishop's Visitation'		19	0d
1637	A shugar loaf and a whole sheep presented to ye judges	1	17	6d'

There were frequent problems from mediaeval times until the Borough boundaries were extended in 1889, because persons living in the Warnership of Pimperne, when was a large part of the western and north-western part of the town, claimed exemption from borough control. People living in this part of the town, which included the west side of West Street, the west side of Salisbury Street, all Bryanston Street, Whitecliff Mill Street and the area north of The Plocks, were outside the Borough and subject to the control of the Court Leet of Pimperne, which in 1547 they were still calling the 'Hundred Law Day'. Among the cases heard at Pimperne on 25 October of that year, under the heading 'Blandford' was the item:

'The Warrender there comes with his whole warren and presents that William Grene (9d) made assault with a bruner upon William Silkrane and drew blood from him thereore and that Gilbert Bastard (4d) remains ad finem for a licence as a tapster (0) And that John Hunt (12d) William Strete (8d) and Robert Stoke (8d) are innkeepers and sell food in their inns at excessive profit in such sales therefore they are at mercy.'
(The fines are shown in brackets)

To be eligible for admission to a seat on the Borough Council before 1889 it was necessary to have property within the borough. This caused problems, because many of the town's leading citizens lived on the west side of West Street and Salisbury Street. It was ultimately agreed that these people could qualify for admission if they constructed upper windows overhanging the footpath. This is why there are so many protruding upper windows in Salisbury Street today on the west side. The constables were also finding it difficult to apprehend wrong-doers for crimes committed in the Borough, as the offenders only had to cross the road into the warnership to escape arrest. The matter was eventually brought before the higher court in Dorchester who ordered:

'That the bailiff and constables of the borough may enter the said warnership and bring before the justices of the peace any disorderly persons they find there. In addition the inhabitants of the warnership are to join with those in the borough in keeping watches and wards as if they were one liberty.'

Orders were also made to the effect that the Borough licensing laws would apply everywhere in the town. The price and quality of beer was strictly controlled and, in 1639, the quarter sessions at Blandford ordered that any innkeeper selling a quart of best beer, and any innkeeper selling two quarts of ordinary beer, for more than one penny, would be fined £1.

The responsibility for carrying out public executions by hanging rested with the Borough, who ordered the gallows to be erected and for the ducking stool to be brought into use when required. The stool was for punishing quarrelsome women, usually referred to as 'scolds'. It was burned in the 1731 fire and never replaced.

The last public execution was in 1741, when William King and Ben Fluel were hanged in the market place for robbing Lady Grace Hayes. Use of the town pillory was discontinued in 1837 when offenders could no longer lawfully be sentenced to occupy it.

Apart from the troubles of the Civil War period, there is no record of any unusual criminal activity in the town in the 17th and 18th centuries, possibly because so much of it went undetected, but there was trouble from time to time with smugglers, who made good use of the river in the course of their activities. In 1778 smugglers entered the town firing their pistols, attacked the house of the Supervisor of Excise and carried off 16 cwt of tea and nine casks of liquor taken by the Excise men at Thorny Down the day before. In 1780 the situation was reversed, as the Excise officer seized 984 gallons of spirits, which had been smuggled into the town, and sold it by auction at Blandford town hall.

A Court of Record functioned in the Borough from 1605 until 1786 for the purpose of dealing with minor disputes and debts not exceeding £10, but the registers indicate that there was practically no business after the 1731 fire. Perhaps Blandford people had their own ways of dealing with these civil matters 'out of court'.

By 1830 the nation had become aware of the general unrest existing in rural areas, largely brought about by improved literacy and education among the labouring classes and a desire for electoral reform. Their plight was made worse by the loss of employment opportunities attributed to the invention of various kinds of farm machinery, land enclosure and low wages for those who did have work. Rioting was frequent, machinery was broken up, ricks were fired and a general insurrection seemed likely. Most of the Dorset estate owners were against making concessions, but Mr E. B. Portman of Bryanston was an exception — he was prepared to offer higher wages, but in so doing incurred the displeasure of others. One of the steps taken was to split the county into divisions. Each division was to take action to ensure the safety of property and persons. Thousands of special constables were enlisted to put down any general revolt. Mr Portman was responsible for the Blandford division and he reported on 27 November 1830 that:

'We are all safe in our division and have organised matters so well that we can assemble 200 armed and mounted and about 2,000 pedestrian special constables ready to resist any mob . . . A troop of Lancers is just come to Blandford . . . I was on horse-back from 10 till 7 yesterday. If you want the aid of our horsemen send to me or to Mr Farquharson and we will be with you in a trice.'

An unknown agitator wrote to Mr Castleman of Wimborne from Blandford in 1830 in the following terms:

'Mr Castleman, Sir, Sunday night your house shall come down to the ground for you are an inhuman monster and we will dash out your brains — Banks and your sett aught to be sent to hell. The Hanley Torches have not forgot you.'

As a result of the measures taken by the magistrates and landowners, the danger of a general peasants' revolt was averted, but the underlying causes remained. It was becoming clear to Parliament that radical reforms were needed to cope with changed conditions,the rise of non-conformity, better educational and travel facilities and the need for improved public health and better housing. During the passage of the various reform bills of the early 1830s, there was considerable further unrest in the countryside due to the opposition of many senior statesmen and Members of Parliament to any major reforms. Large numbers of broadsheets and handbills for and against reform circulated in Blandford and district. Mr Portman was against some of the reforms and so was Rev George Chard, Rector of Blandford Forum. Mr Portman was opposed by the Hon W. F. S. Ponsonby, brother in law of Lord Melbourne, at the next election for Dorset, and Mr Ponsonby won. He was foreman of the grand jury which sat at Dorchester in March

1834 to commit the Tolpuddle martyrs for trial. The jury was heavily loaded against them, as it consisted mostly of local landowners and magistrates anxious to keep the farm labourers in their place.

Matters again came to a head in October 1831, when there were mass demonstrations and rioting aimed at those opposing reform. Lady Fanny Smith, wife of Sir John Smith of The Down House, in a letter to her mother of 18 October 1831, wrote:

'I am sure that if Mr Portman choses to incourage the mob in this manner they will not long confine their depredations to the town. We are all under arms again here and are to fire if anyone offers to break our windows.'

The Rector called in the military to restore order but they could not act as he was not a magistrate. An appeal was then sent by hand to Sir John Smith, who was a magistrate, to come and read the Riot Act. The letter to him claimed that 'the houses of Mr Moore, Mr Smith and Mr Childs are nearly demolished and they are now demolishing Houliston's house'. It is clear that this was the most serious outbreak of public order ever to be experienced in Blandford. The *Morning Herald* of 22 October 1831 reported that the windows of almost every anti-reformer in Blandford had been broken.

Mr Smith and Mr Moore were lawyers, the former town clerk and in charge of the Bishop's registry at Blandford. Their offices were ransacked and the contents removed and thrown into the streets. As a result of this, many old Blandford title deeds are stained by horse dung and many official records of the town were never recovered, some of them documents known to have survived the fire of 1731.

Mr Portman eventually addressed the rioters, who ultimately dispersed. No doubt his status as employer and landlord of many of them, and his good local reputation, were deciding factors.

George Long, Richard Bleathman, William Kent and Thomas Jackson were the ringleaders and were indicated for 'having on the 17 day of October last, with divers other persons, riotously assembled together in the town of Blandford, and begun to demolish and destroy the house of Mr George Moore at Blandford Forum'. Long and Bleathman were sentenced to death and told not to entertain any hopes of mercy, but their sentences were subsequently reduced to terms of imprisonment.

After the Borough became a municipal corporation in 1834, regular petty sessions began to be held in the town hall before the Mayor, who was an ex-officio magistrate during his term of office, and other justices appointed to act for the Blandford Petty Sessional Division. These Petty Sessions replaced the Court Leet, and the last vestiges of manorial custom thereby came to an end. The justices dealt with all matters arising within the town and district covered by their jurisdiction in connection with crime and licensing matters.

Many towns (Wareham is one) still have their annual courts leet and, although they no longer have any legal powers, they do provide a happy annual event with a bit of pomp and ceremony.

In 1836 the town formed its first official paid police force, who were all part-timers. The superintendent was paid £20 a year and the constables 1s 6d per day for four hours duty by day or by night. It was later decided that constables were not needed on duty at night during the summer months. Blandford must have become a law abiding place following the passing of the Reform Acts, but it must be remembered that, although the public were very much at the mercy of wrongdoers, the penalties for those caught were severe. At the beginning of the 19th century there were well over 200 offences for which the death penalty could be imposed, and by 1836 the justices were frequently ordering transportation for life, or for several years, for quite minor offences. The Martyrs of Tolpuddle, the 150th anniversary of whose trial is being observed this year (1984), were at that time still serving their sentences.

The police wages book for the Borough names the first constables as W. Hodges, Abraham Hardy, Samuel Lance and William Horlock. The first superintendent was Francis Davis, who was followed in 1848 by E. Abberline, a shopkeeper, in 1850 by Peter Southey, a stocking and worsted maker, and in 1857 by George Lanning, a dyer. These superintendents also held office as collectors of the market tolls. Their station was originally behind the town hall but, when the corn exchange was built in 1858, it was moved to Sheep Market Hill to premises which are immadiately below the new public library. The name 'Borough Police' can still be observed over the doorway. For a few years this borough force policed the town alongside the Dorset county constabulary, who were responsible for those parts of the town which were not in the Borough. The county force was formed in 1856 and their station in Salisbury Road, built in 1859, is now called 'd'Arcy Court'. The Dorset Female Penitentiary functioned in Salisbury Street for a few years, but the identity of the building is at present uncertain.

The official town guide of 1907 refers to the ancient pillory, which is fortunately still preserved under the town hall, and 'the ancient stocks as well as many weapons of defence used by the borough police and watchmen of bygone age'. These, alas, cannot now be found.

Other civil matters of local importance were dealt with by the parish Vestry, which met regularly either at the church or in the town hall. Until 1834 they were responsible for the administration of the poor law, the enforcement of church attendance, management of the workhouse and other welfare services, the appointment of churchwardens and other parish officers. They were responsible for levying the poor rates and the church rates until these were abolished in the 19th century, and they authorised all church expenditure. The Vestry minutes from 1737 to 1856 are preserved in the County Record Office in Dorchester and are well worth reading. The Vestry employed local surgeons and apothecaries to look after the sick of the parish for a year at a time on a rota basis. The local doctors taking a turn with this work included Malachi Tice (1737), John Muston (1738), Robert Muston (1747), John Browning (1751), Thomas Wilson (1759), John Dansey (1787), Richard Worsley (1790), William Jackson (1803), and Charles Baskett (1810).

In 1741 the Vestry ordered that paupers not wearing their pauper badges would have their allowances stopped. They also ordered Thomas Channing, Duke Harding, Bugg Snook, John Jarvis and Simon Gothard to be sent to the house of correction at the expense of the parish for not maintaining their families. In 1785 they agreed to buy spinning wheels and to employ John Ashman to teach their use to the poor of the town.

It is clear from the various record books, accounts and registers, now in the County Record Office that, for periods prior to 1834, there was frequent uncertainty as to whether certain decisions on matters of law and order should be dealt with by the justices, the Court Leet, the Court of Record, the Borough Council or the Vestry. The Borough Council, for example, often made orders for vagrants to be whipped although they had no authority to make such orders. The principal officers of the various bodies dispensing law and order were often the same persons, who frequently wore the wrong hats and entered their decisions in the wrong books. No real harm was done and, judging by the standards of those days, they acquitted themselves honourably and to the best of their ability.

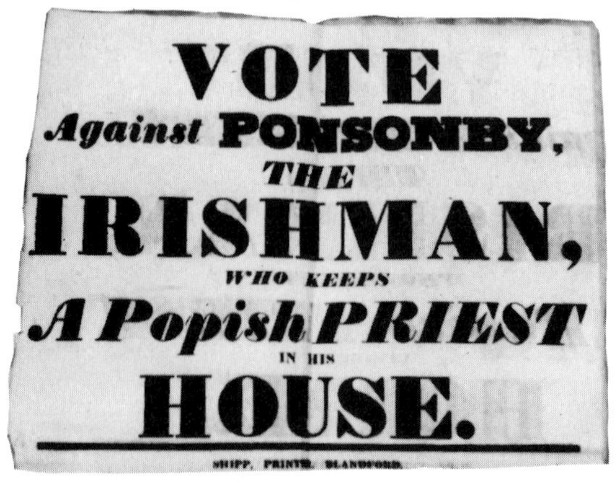

14th Febry 1742

At a Meeting at the Town Hall it is ordered that by the Corporation that Thomas Alan a Vagabond be whipt and that if any Action is brought on the Account the Expenses of defending it shall be borne by the Corporation

W. Milbourne Bayliff

Jo. Bonyfield

Wm: Barland

John: Benjafield Junr

John Thorne

WHEREAS TWO PERSONS

Wearing Dark Great Coats and Hats with *Broad Brims*, were about four o'Clock on Sunday Morning *last* seen near the Hedge between Mill Down and one of Mr. Coward's *Wheat Fields*, who on being discovered immediately ran towards the Lane leading to Shaftesbury; *and whereas*

It is *strongly suspected* that such Two Persons were concerned in *setting Fire to the Ricks* belonging to Mr. Christopher Good, and Mr. John White; Any Person who might at the time before mentioned have seen *Two Men* answering the above Description will *much further the Cause of Justice* by communicating the fact to the Bailiff of the Borough of Blandford.

N. B. The Persons described appeared to be Young Men above the Lower Class of Society.

Blandford, 20th November, 1828.

OPPOSITE: Political broadsheet. 1832. (DCM) ABOVE: Order for whipping of Thomas Alan, a vagrant, 1742; (DRO) BELOW: notice re rick fires, 1828. (DCM)

Novemb: ye 3d: 1673.

Whereas Mr Walter Kerby a Cheife Burges of this Corporation was by the Jurors att the Court Leete (ajorned to the 3 of November 1673 held for this Burrough) presented by the sayd Jurors for sellinge by two halfe pintes made lesse then measure, by meltinge of pitch or such like stuffe into [illegible] to the prejudice of the Inhabitants and disparagement of this Corporation and Towne. Wee therefore the Bayliffe and Burgesses whose names are hereunto subscribed doe therefore by these presents disfranchise the sayd Walter Kerby from beinge any longer a Cheife Burges, and doe discharge him from ye sayd Office and Place dated this tenth day of Novemb: 1673

William [illegible] Bayliffe

Richard [illegible]

Matthew [illegible]

Richard [illegible]

Robt [illegible]

John [illegible]

Christopher [illegible]

Thomas [illegible]

William [illegible]

Order for removal of Walter Kerby from office of chief burgess for selling short measures in his inn, 1673. (DRO)

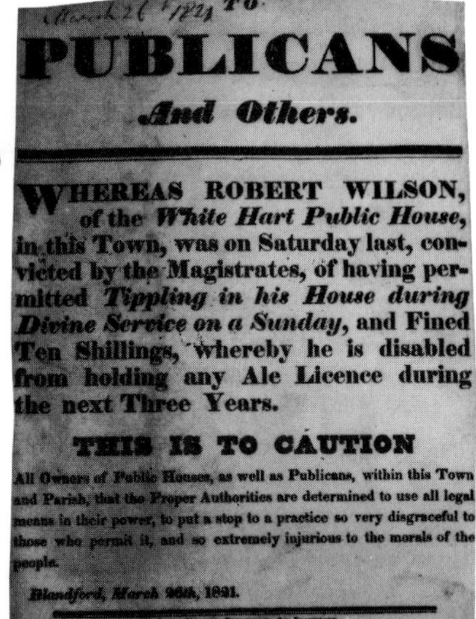

TO

PUBLICANS

And Others.

WHEREAS ROBERT WILSON, of the ***White Hart Public House,*** in this Town, was on Saturday last, convicted by the Magistrates, of having permitted ***Tippling in his House during Divine Service on a Sunday,*** and Fined Ten Shillings, whereby he is disabled from holding any Ale Licence during the next Three Years.

THIS IS TO CAUTION

All Owners of Public Houses, as well as Publicans, within this Town and Parish, that the Proper Authorities are determined to use all legal means in their power, to put a stop to a practice so very disgraceful to those who permit it, and so extremely injurious to the morals of the people.

Blandford, March 26th, 1821.

THE BLANDFORD,

Reform Committee,

Anxious to preserve as far as may be in their power, the property and peace of this *Town and Neighbourhood* from further violation, and deprecating the scenes of tumult, riot and destruction which have already taken place, earnestly intreat the *Inhabitants of this Town and Neighbourhood* to abstain from those *nightly tumultuous assemblages* which have led to these breaches of the peace, and to use all their exertions to prevent others from engaging in the same, convinced that such outrages are *disgraceful to Englishmen* and most injurious to the *Cause of Reform.*

Masters and Parents are particularly requested to use their utmost endeavours to keep their children and servants at home.

BLANDFORD, October 19th, 1831

LEFT: The town pillory, now under Town Hall; (BM) RIGHT: warning to publicans, 1821; (DCM) BELOW: notice re 'Tumultuous Assemblages', 1831. (DCM)

To the Inhabitants of
BLANDFORD
And its Vicinity.

You have this day by your conduct when called on to come forward for the protection of the Public Peace, proved yourselves worthy not only of your native County, but more especially of the Town and neighbourhood wherein you reside. You have this day evinced a promptitude, and a determination, and a courage, (which if persevered in nothing can overcome) to quell a lawless rabble who have of late been infesting the Country, whose only object is to create Disturbances and cause greater Want and greater Misery to many who are now enduring much, by the wilful Destruction of Property and even of the *Actual Necessaries of Life.* You have this day shewn an example which it is to be hoped will speedily spread throughout the County, and will operate not only as a warning to surrounding Districts, but will convince the Incendiary and Insubordinate that they are not at least to cross the Dorsetian Boundary with impunity--- that you are moreover fully prepared at all points to give them a WARM RECEPTION should they have the temerity to appear in this your neighbourhood, and resolved as far as in you lies to preserve both the Peace and the Property of your native Land.

Go on then in the Good Cause you have all this day undertaken, be firm, be active, be vigilant, and above all BE UNITED. Fear not and you will attain the desired end.

Nothing believe me but indisposition prevented my being where my heart was, and where my hand (otherwise) would have been, amongst you at your head.

DOUGLAS W. STUART,

A Special Constable.

FRIDAY EVENING, NOVEMBER 26th, 1830.

SHIPP, PRINTER, BLANDFORD.

ABOVE: Praise for the special constables, 1830; (DCM) OPPOSITE ABOVE: some were returned, some were not; (DCM) BELOW: notice by anti-reformers, 1831. (DCM)

NOTICE.

ALL PERSONS having in their possession any *Parchment* or *Paper Writings*, taken from the *Bishop's Registry* in Blandford or from Mr. SMITH's *Offices*, on the night of Monday the 17th of October last, are requested to deliver the same forthwith to Mr. SMITH.

BLANDFORD, NOVEMBER 3rd, 1831.

Anti-Radical REFORM.

The Inhabitants of BLANDFORD are respectfully informed that a PETITION to both Houses of Parliament will lie for signature at *Mr. Shipp's Library, on Monday next and four following days*, in order to afford an opportunity to those who are attached to our *Glorious Constitution*, to declare that while they are by no means averse to any sound and temperate measure for PARLIAMENTARY REFORM that may be devised, they cannot but view with horror and dismay, the dangerous and unconstitutional plan now proposed to be adopted; the direct tendency of which is in their opinion to overthrow the just equilibrium so happily established in KING, LORDS, and COMMONS, and by sweeping away so many vested rights and removing so many Members, (no less than Eleven being taken away from their own County) to be at once unjust and tyrannical, and likely to involve this great and happy Country in confusion and anarchy.

***Blandford, March 5th*, 1831.**

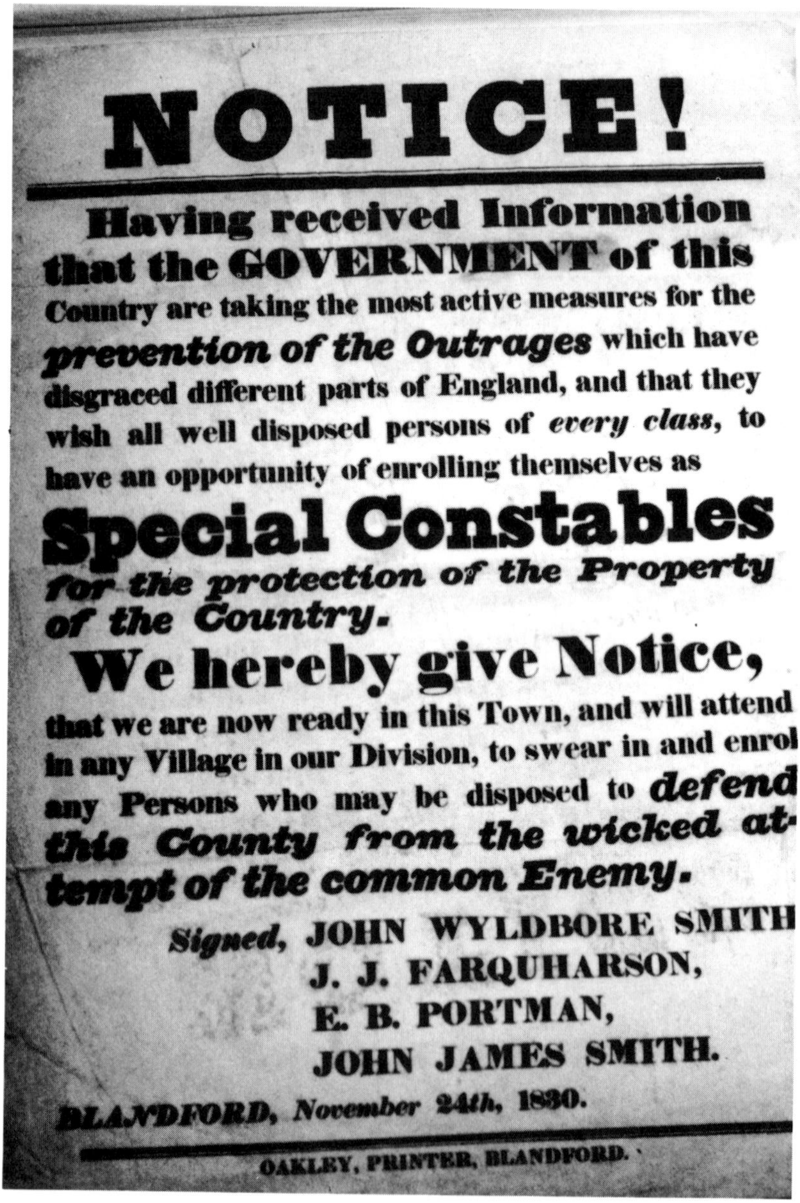

NOTICE!

Having received Information that the GOVERNMENT of this Country are taking the most active measures for the *prevention of the Outrages* which have disgraced different parts of England, and that they wish all well disposed persons of *every class*, to have an opportunity of enrolling themselves as

Special Constables

for the protection of the Property of the Country.

We hereby give Notice,

that we are now ready in this Town, and will attend in any Village in our Division, to swear in and enrol any Persons who may be disposed to *defend this County from the wicked attempt of the common Enemy.*

Signed, **JOHN WYLDBORE SMITH**
J. J. FARQUHARSON,
E. B. PORTMAN,
JOHN JAMES SMITH.

***BLANDFORD,* *November 24th,* 1830.**

OAKLEY, PRINTER, BLANDFORD.

Notice of readiness of special constables, 1830. (DCM)

50 POUNDS

REWARD.

Whereas, Three several Fires have occurred within the last fortnight in the Parish of Blandford St. Mary, in the County of Dorset., which there is too much reason to believe were the work of an Incendiary.

The above Reward will be given to any Person or Persons giving such information, privately or otherwise, as to either of the said Fires as may lead to the discovery of the perpetrator.

The above Reward will only be paid on the Conviction of the Offender.

Dated, Down House, Sep. 4, 1850. J. W. SMITH, BART.

W. SHIPP, PRINTE[illegible]DFORD.

DORSET

ANY PERSON WILFULLY INJURING
ANY PART OF THIS COUNTY BRIDG
WILL BE GUILTY OF FELONY AN
UPON CONVICTION LIABLE TO BE
TRANSPORTED FOR LIFE
BY THE COURT
7&8 GEO 4 C30 S13 T FOOKS

ABOVE: Reward offer 1850; (DCM) BELOW: penal notice erected on Blandford bridge in the 1830s. (SJ)

TO THE

BURGESSES

OF THE BOROUGH OF

BLANDFORD FORUM

GENTLEMEN,

The proper determination of the Corporation to prevent the infringement of *public decency and good order* by *improper* Shows and Exhibitions in the Market-Place, has given rise to an organized movement to prevent the re-election of those Councillors who prominently advocated the needed reform.

An active canvass is being made in favor of those persons nominated to fill the places of those going out of office, and it will be for you as Burgesses of the Borough to say whether the Gentlemen who have had the moral courage to advocate *public decency and good order*, and who are eligible for re-election, shall be replaced by those nominated in opposition to them.

Say, gentlemen, which shall it be, Public Decency and Good Order, or Public indifference to either?

A BURGESS.

Blandford, Oct. 31st, 1862.

W. SHIPP, PRINTER, BLANDFORD.

Notice re indecent shows at Blandford, 1862. (DCM)

ABOVE: Former Borough police station on Sheepmarket Hill; (SJ)
BELOW: old County Police station in Salisbury Road. (SJ)

ABOVE: Arms of Berkeley Portman of Bryanston; (BM) BELOW: Blandford firemen, 1915.

Care of the Poor

For many centuries the care of the poor of the town, and persons in need passing through it, were the most onerous tasks of the leaders. In early mediaeval times there was no legal obligation upon anyone to render help to another, and punishments for begging by people who were able to work were severe. The Borough of Blandford did what it could by making payments to those in need from its small income and from charitable funds which it administered. Christian Crouch, to choose one example from the chamberlain's accounts, was kept by the Borough for 59 weeks from June 1598 and was supplied with three pairs of shoes, a waistcoat, two woollen aprons, a coat and two coifs (hats of some sort). Numerous payments were made for the benefit of those living in the almshouses, and to assist exceptionally gifted poor boys to attend their grammar school.

In the 50 years or so following the dissolution of the monasteries, which for centuries had born the major brunt of caring for the poor, Blandford saw a serious and rapidly increasing influx of travellers from other districts seeking alms and employment. The situation was getting out of hand by 1601 when an act, known as the Elizabethan poor law, put the responsibility for caring for the poor, the sick and the infirm upon the parish, and this remained the basis of our poor law for nearly 250 years. The overseers of the poor were empowered to raise rates and to expend the money for the relief of those in need. Although help was given to those in need passing through the town, the overseers would not relieve people intending to prolong their stays, unless they were legally settled here. In 1780, for example, Mary Harvey, a Blandford girl, had named John Hardyt as the father of her baby. Hardy, being a Wimborne man, was not settled in Blandford, and was promptly arrested by the parish constable and placed in the town lock-up under guard until he agreed to marry the girl. On this occasion the overseers paid for the licence, the ring, the reception at the White Hart and the men who had arrested and guarded him. He and his new family were then moved out of the town to become chargeable on the Wimborne overseers, where he was settled, until he was able to support his family. Blandford overseers deemed this expense to be justified, as they thereby avoided the possibility of being liable, perhaps for several years, for the maintenance of the family.

When Sir F. M. Eden visited Blandford in the 1790s to collect material for his great survey of the state of the poor, he found a shocking state of affairs here, with farm labourers' wages only 6s or 7s a week. He found 36 inmates in the parish workhouse and more than 100 others receiving regular parish relief. He also commented 'the rapid rise of the poor rate in this parish is generally attributed to the high price of provisions, the smallness of wages, and the consolidation of small farms and consequent depopulation of villages'.

As a general indication of the scale of payments and receipts the income from the Blandford poor rates rose from £357 13 4d in 1776 to £828 10 0d in 1785 to meet increasing calls for help.

The overseers had to comply with the legal requirement that paupers, men, women and children, should wear a badge with the letters 'PB' on their outer clothing. The 'P' represented 'pauper' and the 'B' Blandford. Eventually this requirement was not enforced, as some of the overseers had risen to be prosperous merchants and tradesmen from families who had themselves known hard times and were perhaps 'PB's'.

The accounts of the overseers of the poor make fascinating reading, with a story of human suffering behind each item; from the 17th v 18th century registers:

		£	s	d
'1728	Gave a poor woman heavy with child a shilling to go away		1	0
1735	Richd Bennett — thatching ye hutts (temporary homes of fire victims)		6	6
1736	Richd Blythewood for bleeding Ann Cox at 2 several times		1	0
1738	Paid Old Hart for looking after ye man in yr smallpox		12	0
	Removing a woman by order to Brianstone			
	Paid two midwives for searching above and below		10	0
1739	Paid for ye cure of John Pottles wife of ye itch		1	6
1742	Poor woman with pass going from Portsmouth to Cornwall		1	0
	Paid a months keeping Mary Shittler at the madhouse due 18th inst	1	0	0
1744	'Pd the woman who was taken in travail on the bridge			10
1745	Pd for 4 doz and half badges (pauper badges)		11	6
1746	Pd Mr Jno Muston for looking after sick in the Parish (he was the parish Doctor)	10	0	0

		£	s	d
1748	Francis Payne his leg being broke		6	6
1749	Gave Bug Snook			6
1756	Paid for sweeping ye chimneys of the poor		2	6
1760	Paid Dr Dansey for cutting of Saml Tuckers leg	6	6	0
1761	One yrs window tax for the workhouse	1	19	0
1763	Sent by Eliz Ball to ye Bath Ospatal	3	0	0
1775	Paid for carrying Sall Bead's child yt was left at my door, back again			6
1782	Paid for militia mens wives	46	6	0
1785	The woman for instructing the workhouse children to spin — 1 month		12	0
1786	Paid at the Red Lion for a por family detained by the snow		6	6
1814	Attendance on James Parsons taken out of the water		15	0
1816	Mr Kendall for crying (Town Bell-man)		1	0'

Blandford's first workhouse, or 'house of industry' as it was sometimes called, was acquired in 1759; it was described as 'a house with a good outlett situate in the East Street'. This was on the north side opposite what is now known as Nightingale's Court. The able-bodied inmates, including the men and the children, were trained to make buttons. This button making industry became the largest in the town in the 18th and 19th centuries, and the proceeds of sale helped to mitigate the amounts raised from the poor rates.

William Holloway, the Winterborne Whitechurch-born poet, in his *The peasant's fate* published in 1802, included the following description of conditions in a workhouse. One wonders if he had seen conditions in Blandford:

> 'A hopeless race, that own yon bleak abode,
> Of Grief and Care, beside the public road,
> Propp'd are whose leaning walls, whose hanging door
> Drags heavy, jarring on the earthen floor
> Keen thro' the shatte'd casements cold winds blow,
> The half-stripp'd roof admits the whirling snow;
> Scarce, on the gloomy hearth, on lingering spark
> The cricket cheers, or gilds his cavern dark;
> While, shivering round, the wretched inmates stand, . . .
> A ragged, meagre, pale, dejected band!
> Here is the man who wealthy days has seen;
> Here is the widow, . . . once the village queen; . . .
> Here too, the damsel, who, in guardless hour,
> Fell a sad victim to Seductions pow'r! . . .
> Curst be the villain, whose insidious art
> Tainted her virgin purity of heart,

Then left her, thus, to shame, reproach, and grief,
Sure only in the grave to find relief: . . .
Here orphans bend to Poverty's hard laws,
Whose fathers perish'd in their Country's cause!
Wives, . . . anxious wives! for distant husbands mourn
In vain anticipating their return!
Mothers, of their last duteous sons bereft,
Without one hope, or consolation left;
With numbers more, whose tale but to disclose,
Would swell "the catalogue of human woes."'

In 1813, after several meetings, Mr Portman, Mr Malachi Tice, a local medical man, and other leading citizens lent money for the erection of new premises in East Street. An entry in the churchwardens' accounts under 18 June 1814 reads 'paid the ringers at the laying of the corner stone of the workhouse 00.08.00.'.

As the result of the Poor Law Amendment Act of 1834 the responsibility for caring for the poor passed from the parish officers to a Board of Guardians elected by the parishes in the district. The Blandford Union comprised 34 parishes.

The census of 1851 lists over 200 inmates in the old East Street workhouse, so one can imagine what things were like. One notable inmate was a blind girl, Caroline Watts who, according to the census, was 25 years of age. She was the authoress of *Poems by a Blind Girl* published by Peter & Galpin, London, in 1864.

By 1857 it was realised that conditions as they were in East Street could no longer be tolerated, as the guardians were having to run a mixed estalishment with sick, aged, feeble-minded and orphaned persons unsegregated in the same accommodation. The guardians ultimately erected a new workhouse in Salisbury Road on land made available by Lord Portman. The contract was given to Mr T. B. Miles of Shaftesbury, and the cost was £8,000. These new premises were opened in 1858 and provided a better quality of life for the residents. The census of 1911 shows 9 officers in attendance at the workhouse to look after 76 residents.

In the 1880s there were still plenty of hungry people in Blandford. The parish magazine of 1889 refers to the Mayor having consented to the opening of the soup kitchen at the back of the Corn Exchange, and inviting donations towards the cost.

Early in the present century there was a good deal of abject poverty in the town and, in spite of much help from various organisations, the standard of living of many was such as would not be tolerated today.

From all accounts, Blandford workhouse had a good reputation, particularly with tramps or 'roadsters' as they were called. In one month between December 1928 and January 1929 the total number of vagrants admitted to the Blandford Union casual wards was 549, including 22 women and 8 children — Christmas in the workhouse was probably the attraction.

In 1929 the County Council took over responsibility from the Board of Guardians and it remained with the Council until the welfare state, and social security, arrived after the 1939/45 war.

The Salisbury Road workhouse became known as Castleman House and, after much of it was demolished and new dwellings erected on the site in the 1970s, the Castleman Homes.

The date of erection of Blandford's first almshouses is not known. In 1564 John Swayne left £20 'for the use of the almshouses'. In 1568 the town invested ten pounds in a national lottery and the Chamberlain's account book indicates that the winnings would be used on repairs to the bridge, the school house, the almshouses, the town houses and the streets. His accounts for 1581 note the rebuilding of the almshouses, on a site west of the church, with a chapel, for which a stool and table were bought for five shilling and six pence. These became known as the church almshouses because of their close proximity to the church, but all responsibility for them seemed to be accepted by the Borough. In 1583 there is an interesting note of one of the sources of benefit it reads:

'There is in Mr Swains lands one acre of ground belonging to the almshouse lying near a thorn bush in ye ffield above Whytlye mill for which he payeth every third year 100 faggots to the almspeople.'

In 1617 the Borough paid for 1,000 faggots for the almshouse at a cost of £3 and 20 shillings a year for prayers to be read. The almshouse minute books and accounts go back to 1631 and record elections to the almhouses, details of income and expenditure and set out the rules applicable to the inmates. They were not allowed to have children to live with them, they could not take lodgers, marry, be whoremongers or fornicators and must obey the orders of the steward and constables at all times.

The almshouses were destroyed in the 1731 fire and rebuilt on a different site north of the parish church between the school house and the Rectory. They served the town until 1926 when, due to their state of repair, they were replaced by new dwellings erected in Park Road. The old almshouses were for a number of years after 1926 used as a public bath house. Only the entrance portico now remains.

Another group of almshouses was erected in Salisbury Street in 1682 for the elderly of Blandford and Pimperne. These were the foundation of George Ryves, who had lived in his younger days at Damory Court, Blandford, but who was at the time of the foundation living at Ranston. By his Will of 1684 he endowed these almshouses, which he called a 'Gerontocomium', with substantial income and appointed trustees, but the day-to-day running was left to the bailiffs of the Borough and the stewards appointed by them. Each inmate of the Ryves almshouses was required to wear a badge of a silver greyhound, the Ryves family crest, and each would receive two shillings and sixpence a week and 'a gowne or other garment, a peece of grey cloathe or searge'. Any surplus income was to be used to apprentice poor boys. The almshouses are still occupied, with the number of occupants reduced from the original ten to five in order to provide better accommodation.

Although they were never almshouses, mention should be made of the great benefit to the town arising from the provision by the first Viscount Portman, of the cottage homes in Shorts Lane, which he named Harewood Place, his wife being Lady Emma Lascelles, daughter of the second Earl of Harewood, and The Barnes Homes in Salisbury Road by John Iles Barnes, the latter erected in 1909 in memory of his brother Philip Abraham Barnes who had been Mayor of Blandford seven times. It should be made clear that the present occupiers of the almshouses and homes mentioned now contribute substantially to their own maintenance, and are no longer in the category of 'almshouse people' of the bad old days.

Ryves Almshouses. (BM)

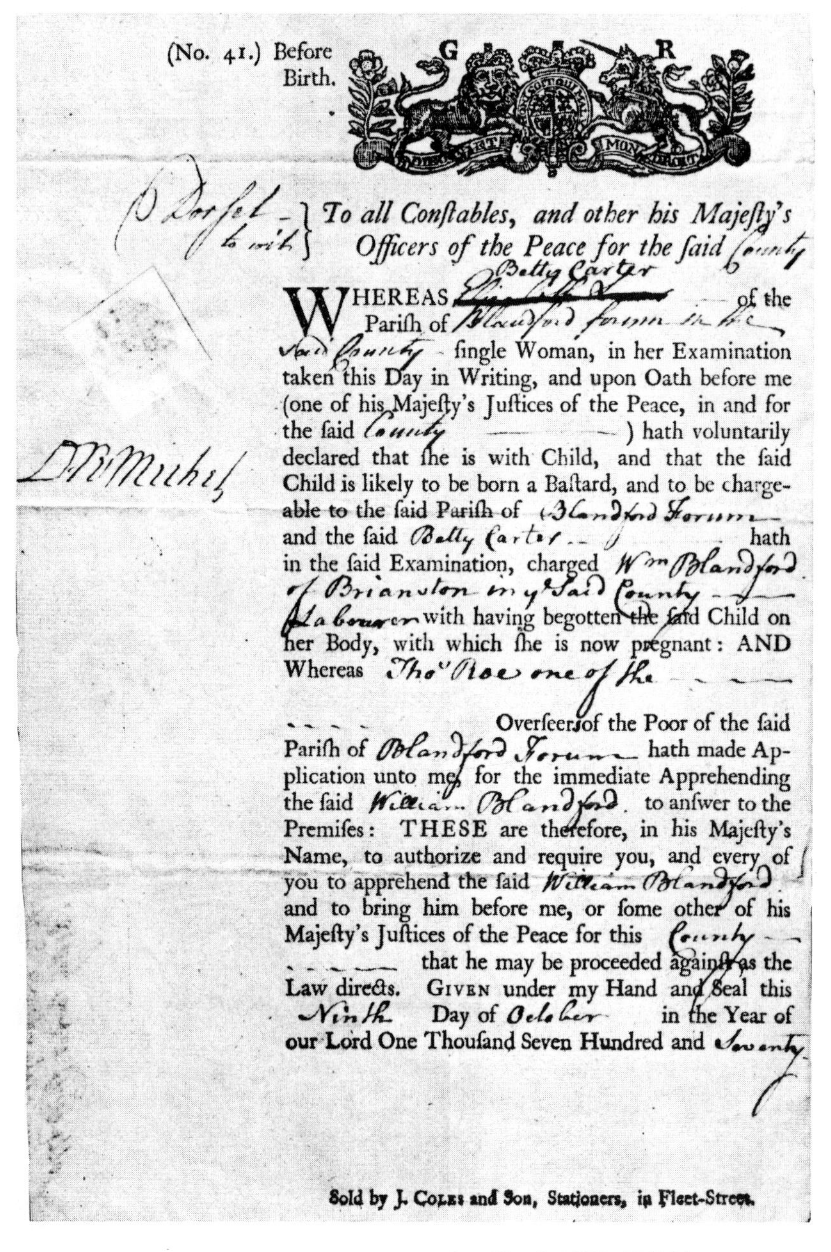
(No. 41.) Before Birth.

G R

Dorset to wit } To all Constables, and other his Majesty's Officers of the Peace for the said County

WHEREAS Betty Carter of the Parish of Blandford Forum in the said County single Woman, in her Examination taken this Day in Writing, and upon Oath before me (one of his Majesty's Justices of the Peace, in and for the said County) hath voluntarily declared that she is with Child, and that the said Child is likely to be born a Bastard, and to be chargeable to the said Parish of Blandford Forum and the said Betty Carter hath in the said Examination, charged Wm Blandford of Brianston in ye said County Labourer with having begotten the said Child on her Body, with which she is now pregnant: AND Whereas Thos Roe one of the Overseers of the Poor of the said Parish of Blandford Forum hath made Application unto me for the immediate Apprehending the said William Blandford to answer to the Premises: THESE are therefore, in his Majesty's Name, to authorize and require you, and every of you to apprehend the said William Blandford and to bring him before me, or some other of his Majesty's Justices of the Peace for this County that he may be proceeded against as the Law directs. GIVEN under my Hand and Seal this Ninth Day of October in the Year of our Lord One Thousand Seven Hundred and Seventy

D. Michel

Sold by J. Coles and Son, Stationers, in Fleet-Street.

Order for arrest of William Blandford, 1770. (DRO)

LEFT: Plaque on Ryves Almshouses; (BM) RIGHT: William Holloway. (BM)

ABOVE: Salisbury Road showing YMCA, the Fair Field and Union workhouse, c1900; (SJ) BELOW: entrance to church almshouses. (BM)

Began 17th Decemr 1770		Mon	Tues	Wednes	Thurs	Fry	Satur	Mon	Tues	Wednes	Thurs	Fry	Satur
Eliz Jessop	Dozs	7	7	7	7	7	7	7		3½	7	7	7
Rebecca Osmond	Dozs	10	10	10	10	10	10	10		5	10	10	10
Ann Rain	Dozs	10	10	10	10	10	10	10		5	10	10	10
Jno Jenkins	Dozs	sick	Do	Do	Do	Do	Do	Do		Do	Do	Do	Do
Elisha Osmond	Dozs	9	9	9	9	9	9	9		4½	9	9	9
Robt Lance		ringing	9	9	9	9	9	9		4½	9	ringing [illegible]	9
Sarah Mitchel Juner	Dozs	7	7	7	7	7	7	7		3½	7	7	7
Richd Hussh	Dozs	7	7	7	7	7	7	7		3½	7	7	7
Sarah Hanney		sick	7	7	7	7	7	7		3½	7	7	7
Catron Sheperd	Dozs	5½	5½	5½	5½	5½	5½	5½		2-9	5½	5½	5½
Mary Osmond	Dozs	5	5	5	5	5	5	5		2½	5	5	5
Willm Lance	Dozs	5	5	5	5	5	5	5		2½	5	5	5
Thos Mitchel	Dozs	4½	4½	4½	4½	4½	4½	4½		2-3	4½	4½	4½
Eliz Hanney	Dozs	4	4	4	4	4	4	4	Christmas Day	2	4	4	4
Lucy Kettle	Dozs	5	5	5	5	5	5	5		2½	5	5	5
Mary Wyatts		washing	Do	3½	3½	3½	sick	washing		washing	3	3½	3½
Ann Lowes	Dozs	6	6	6	6	6	6	6		3	6	6	6
Sarah Mitchel Sener													

Workhouse Master's record of buttons made by inmates in a period of 11 days in 1770. (DRO)

Aprils the 16 1810

Jentlman

I Joseph Pain do Begg the Favour
of your Honours to make a Little
a Dishon to my wickly Pay for my
Louance from your Honnours and my
Labour which I Bring in is not
anuf to Soport my Family Only Low
me While Bread is so Dear for I am
Getting in Dett Every wick I hope
your honners will help to so Port me
a ~~Little~~ to keep me from being more
Troubelsom for I have 5 under 11 years
So I Remain your Troubelsom
Servant J Pain

Answd

Letter from Joseph Pain to Overseers of the poor, 1810. (DRO)

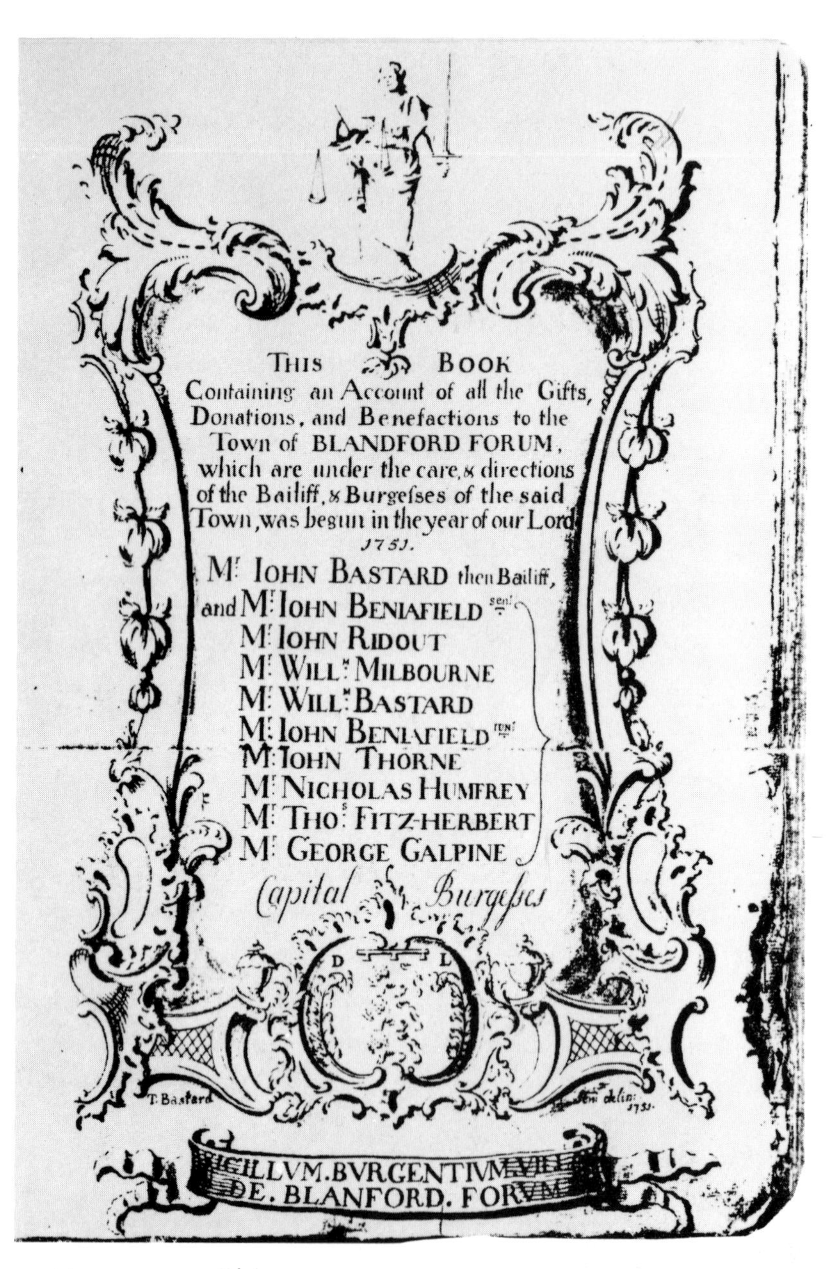
THIS BOOK
Containing an Account of all the Gifts,
Donations, and Benefactions to the
Town of BLANDFORD FORUM,
which are under the care, & directions
of the Bailiff, & Burgeſses of the said
Town, was begun in the year of our Lord
1751.
Mr. IOHN BASTARD then Bailiff,
and Mr. IOHN BENIAFIELD senr.
Mr. IOHN RIDOUT
Mr. WILLm. MILBOURNE
Mr. WILLm. BASTARD
Mr. IOHN BENIAFIELD iunr.
Mr. IOHN THORNE
Mr. NICHOLAS HUMFREY
Mr. THOs. FITZ-HERBERT
Mr. GEORGE GALPINE
Capital Burgeſses
T. Bastard
delin: 1751.
SIGILLVM.BVRGENTIVM.VILL
DE. BLANFORD. FORVM

Title page of Blandford Corporation Charity Book, 1751, designed by Thomas Bastard; (DRO) OPPOSITE ABOVE: Blandford Mendicity Society was formed shortly after this, (DCL) and BELOW: Blue-coat boys at play 1930. (SJ)

Blandford, Dorset.

A proposed Society for the Relief of distressed Travellers, and the Detection of Vagrants, and Impostors.

A general Meeting of the Inhabitants of Blandford and its Vicinity, for the purpose of taking into consideration the establishment of a Society as above, will be held at the TOWN HALL *of Blandford, on Monday August 2nd.* 1819.

At ONE o'Clock.

HENRY WHITE, Bailiff.

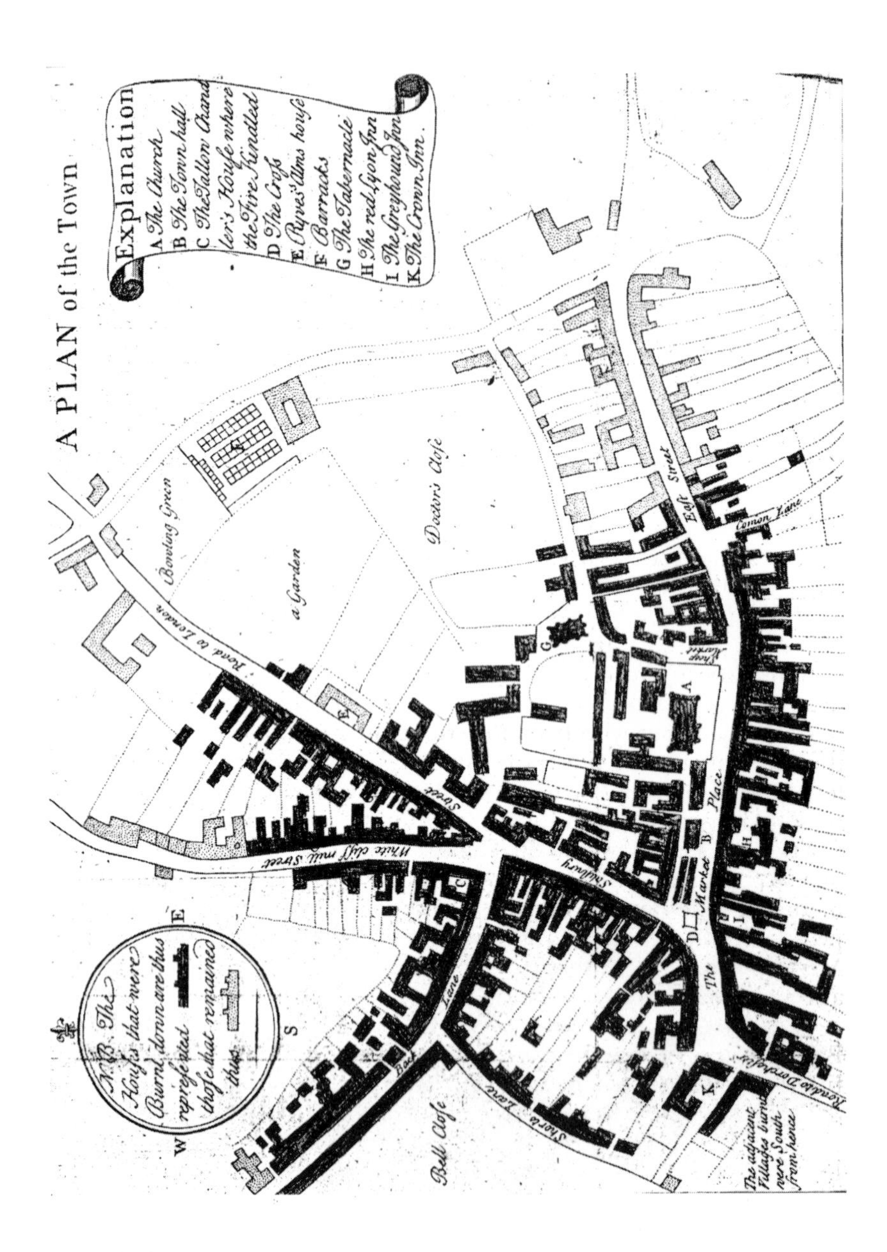

Malachi Blake's plan of 1732 showing extent of the 1731 fire. (BM)

Fires and Bastards

More has been written about Blandford's sufferings from disastrous fires than any other aspect of its long and chequered history, but some account of them is essential to a proper record of the town.

The first fire of which we know occurred in or about 1564. The earliest record occurs in the Borough chamberlain's accounts for that year. The fire destroyed the old guildhall, the almshouses, the school and private property in what is now central Blandford, but there is no account of loss of life. It looks as though the old records were lost in this fire as those extant commence in 1564. The following minute is recorded:

'This day is ordered by the assent of the whole town that whatsoever he be which in this town after this present day that having any chimney in his house to be on fire, that he shall lose to the maintenance of the town three shillings and fourpence to be levied by distress by the bailiff And if the bailiff do not levy it then he shall lose to the town for every default Five shillings.'

The next big fire was in 1677, and we do not know a lot about this one, except that 33 families were made homeless. An apeal was made for relief and this resulted in money being raised by various persons and parishes over a wide area. A church brief issuing from Mere in Wiltshire in that year produced 11 shillings and 4 pence and reads (in more modern English).

'A brief published for relief of 33 families in the Parish of Blandford Forum in the county of Dorset by means of a lamentable fire that happened there on May the 24th last past, sustained loss to the value of £3092 8 0. Collected 11 4d.'

On 9 July 1713 the lower part of East Street was destroyed by fire. Little is known about the extent of the damage or whether there were any lives lost. The historian John Hutchins attributed the fire to the work of a malicious person.

The next and last great fire started on the afternoon of 4 June 1731 and destroyed the parish church, the almshouses near the church, the school, the town hall, and all but about a dozen of the town's houses, public buildings and business premises. Parts of Blandford St Mary and Bryanston near Blandford bridge were also destroyed. Properties not destroyed were the Old House in the

Close, the Ryves almshouses, Dale House and other buildings at the upper end of Salisbury Street and Whitecliff Mill Street, with several between Stour House and the eastern end of East Street, being largely those which had been rebuilt after the fire of 1713. The 1731 fire effectively hastened the end of an epidemic of smallpox which had been raging in Blandford at the time. Fortunately a full contemporary account of the 1731 fire was written by Rev Malachi Blake, a dissenting minister at Blandford, who lost his own meeting house and his home in the disaster. His account, reprinted in 1981, is readily available.

The Blandford parish registers show 12 persons (3 men and 9 women) as 'burnt and interred' on 4 June. There were 37 more burials between then and 13 July, including five children. It can be assumed that several of these were smallpox victims, and others elderly people whose deaths were hastened by the effects of the fire. The numbers buried are far in excess of the normal numbers for such a short period.

It was necessary, in order to maintain the trade and importance of the town, for quick action to be taken towards rebuilding, and an act of Parliament was obtained authorising the necessary measures. This received the Royal assent on 1 July 1732. It provided for the setting up of a special Court of Record 'to hear and determine all differences and demands whatsoever which have arisen or may arise between proprietors, landlords, tenants or late occupiers of any of the houses or buildings burnt down or otherwise demolished or damaged by reason of the said fire'. The proceedings of this court are preserved in the Dorset County Record Office and show decisions made in a total of 42 cases heard in the course of seventeen sessions held between August 1732 and August 1740. It authorised the removal of various bottle-necks and obstructions in the town. The market place was cleared of obstructions, including the old Town Hall, the Shambles, and four cottages known as Middle Row. The Market Cross, which was probably of stone and substantial enough to give cover to several stalls, was awkwardly placed at the junction of the Market Place with West Street and Salisbury Street, and was removed, but not on the authority of the rebuilding Act. The map accompanying Malachi Blake's account of the fire damage does not show the Cross as destroyed.

The cost of rebuilding was supplemented by private donations, including £1,000 from George II, £200 from Queen Caroline, £100 from the Prince of Wales and varying amounts from peers, commoners, universities, churches, towns and cities throughout the country. Old Blandfordian William Wake, then Archbishop of Canterbury, chipped in £100 and Drury Lane Theatre put on a play 'for the unhappy sufferers from the late fire'. The rebuilding Act placed all the available funds at the disposal of the following trustees: The Honourable George Doddington, Sir William Napier, Sir William Chapple, Sir James Thornhill, George Chaffin, Edmund Moreton Pleydell, William Portman, Henry Drax, George Trenchard, Richard Bingham, Robert Henley, William Churchill, Robert Mitchell, Walter Ridout and Robert Snooke. The Act also laid down that all rebuilding should be in brick with lead, slate or tile for roofing.

At the time of the fire, John, Thomas and William Bastard were in business in Blandford as architects, builders and joiners. They had learned their trades from their father, Thomas Bastard. They had all had considerable experience and had played a big part in the country-house building boom of that time. Their father had built Charlton Marshall church and the rectory at Spetisbury, and had carried out major works at Winterborne Stickland and Almer churches.

Thomas junior died a few weeks after this fire and John and William, who had a good reputation locally, were well equipped to undertake for the Trustees the planning for, and supervision of, the rebuilding of the town, and to do the major part of the work themselves. That they did the job to the satisfaction of the town is evidenced by the fact that John subsequently held office as bailiff five times and William twice.

John Bastard compiled a detailed and priced inventory of the losses of everybody in the town including the Corporation and the church. The total loss was assessed at £86,882 13 3½d. Bastard & Co. were the largest private losers, their own claim amounting to £3,709 10 4d.

John and William organised the design and rebuilding of the Borough of Blandford's own properties including the town hall, the grammar school and the almshouses, and erected a temporary church which was called the Tabernacle; the site still has this name. Their original design for the church included a spire, and they were vexed in later years that, for financial reasons, a cupola was substituted. They referred to it as 'a short lived wooden top' but it is still there.

The Corporation's losses included the town hall £600, the old church almshouses £150, the school house £524, the fire engine house and market house where all the hurdles and market equipment were kept £68, four fire engines £100, fire crooks £3, the butchers' shambles £30, three dozen leather buckets £6, 'jayle' house £135, pillory, stocks and ducking stool £18, goods £24. In connection with the rebuilding of the town hall they seem to have conferred with others. Sir James Thornhill's design for Blandford town hall is remarkably like the erection finally decided upon so far as its outward appearance is concerned.

It is obvious that the Bastard brothers could not personally have executed all this work from their own resources in so short a time, without sub-contracting a lot of the work to other builders and specialist craftsmen such as stone masons and plasterers, but they did retain overall control and were the real town planners of the day. Any records they may have kept, other than in respect of their own properties, have not so far come to light. There is no doubt that they rebuilt the Red Lion Inn, the Greyhound Inn and the magnificent house, half of which is in the Market Place and half in East Street, in which these bachelors themselves lived. The house never had a name but is usually identified as 'Bastards' House'. The stone archway beneath, which survived the fire, led to their stores and workshops, stabling and coach-house, the latter now in use as the town's museum.

Many of the town's private houses were rebult by contractors other than the Bastard brothers, partly to minimise the inconvenience of having to be without a home, and partly because compensation under the rebuilding Act could not be claimed if it had not been commenced within the time limits laid down. It is clear from the Bastard brothers' plan, and the schedule of claims, that most of the houses were rebuilt on their original foundations and that a large number were only partly damaged. The claim in respect of Eagle House in Whitecliff Mill Street, for example, was for £78 only, and many of the others were for quite small amounts compared with what it would have cost for a complete rebuilding. A large number of residents were able to continue living in the less damaged parts of their houses and outbuildings. Sixty temporary dwellings only were erected at the top of Damory Street, to accommodate those who were completely homeless.

John Bastard's books make it clear that the work to their own properties was not completed until 1760, and he commemorated the event by erecting the fire monument in the market place, originally as a water pump for use in any future fire which might occur. This was built in Portland stone and converted into a drinking fountain in 1899.

A Borough Council minute of 1766 records a resolution to rebuild the Market Cross. It refers to it as being 'the place where traders exposed for sale pig meat, fish, pastry-cook goods, cheese and bacon'. It also mentions that the temporary stands used by the vendors of these goods at the Greyhound and other places were inconvenient and 'prejudicial and detrimental to the users of the said markets'.

It is difficult to put any precise date on many of the town's Georgian houses. Some were bult immediately after the fire and others in the 1740s, '50s and '60s and, later, by the nephews of John and William Bastard, who succeeded to the business on their uncles' retirement. It seems that the Bastard family did well out of the rebuilding and became gentlemen of means with their own armorial bearings. One thing is certain; the Bastards, and those who worked under them, produced a beautiful and unique Georgian town, now protected as a conservation area and a 'must' for all students of architecture.

In 1738 William Knapp wrote an anthem 'to be sung at Blandford on 4 June every year to commemorate a terrible fire that afflicted the town on that date in the year 1731'. It was contained in a set of new psalm-tunes and anthems published by him at Poole, which ran to seven later editions between 1741 and 1770. It has not been sung at Blandford within living memory, and the Blandford Forum Museum and the Director of Music at the parish church would like to see a copy.

The 17th century 'Old House', a survivor of the 1731 fire. (SJ)

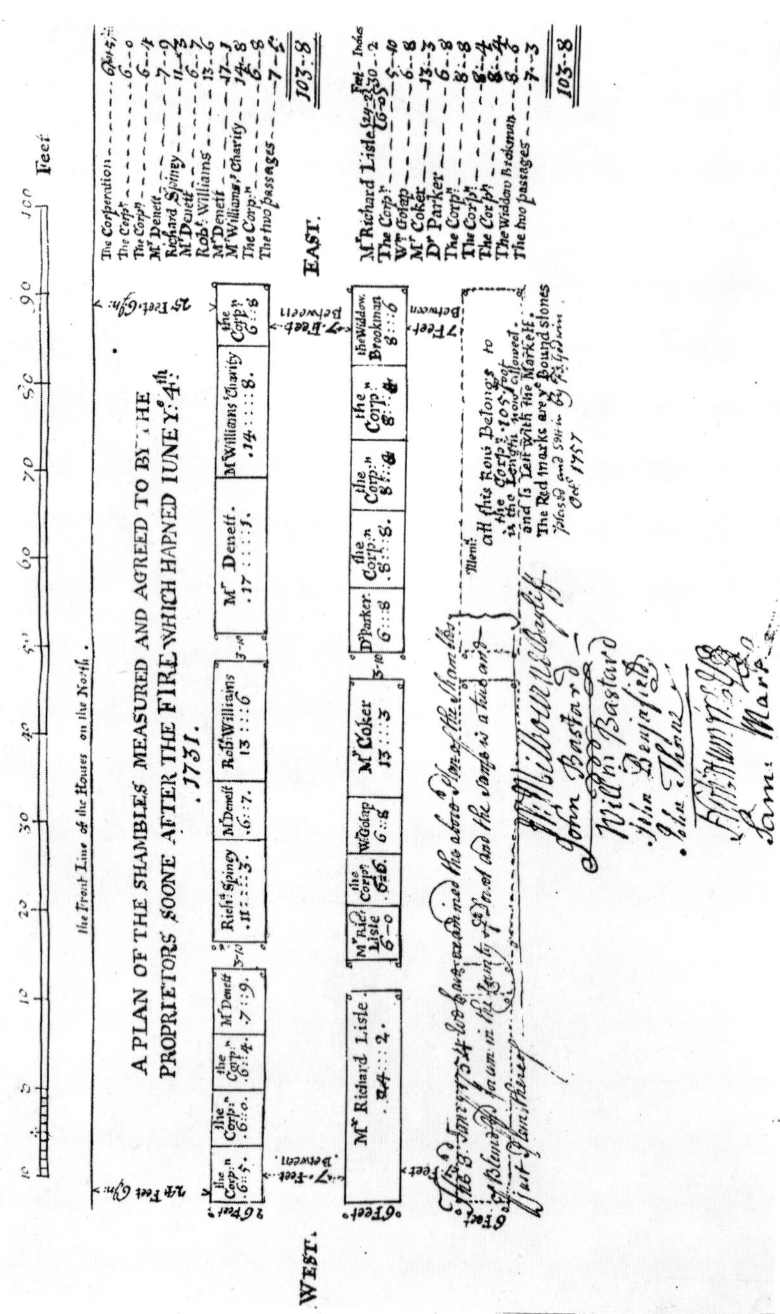

Plan showing the tenants and occupiers of stalls in the Market Place at the time of the 1731 fire. (DRO)

Blandford 20 May, 1735.

Reverend Sir.

SOME time ago, a Letter was ſent you Subſcribed by ſome of your Reverend Brethren, of the Number of thoſe choſen Truſtees, to promote the Rebuilding the Pariſh Church of Blandford, *to deſire of you, to make a Collection in your Pariſh, towards carrying on that pious Work. The generous Encouragement which has been given by ſome, has very much anſwered our Expectations and determined our making a begining this Spring, and God be thank'd, the Building is now happily advancing. This good Reception our Endeavours has met with, from ſome of our pious Neighbours, gives us great Hopes, that we ſhall not want the kind Aſſiſtance of ſuch as have not already ſhewn their Zeal, for the Advancement of this Work. As we have not (Reverend Sir,) had any Anſwer from you, to the above mentioned Letter, we thought proper to addreſs this to you, to intreat the Favour of you, to make a return of what has been given by your Pariſh, (if any Collection has been made by you,) or if none has been made, to let the good People under your Care know that this good Work is now happily begun, and to ſend their Benefactions to Mr.* John Gannett Junior, *of this Place, as ſoon as it ſuits your Conveniency. There appear to us, ſo many peculiar Circumſtances, to preſs your Encouragement of this Charitable Work, that we perſwade our ſelves, nothing farther need be added by us, to prevail with you, to lend your helping Hand. We are*

Reverend Sir,

your most Humble Servants.

William Benjafield.	*Robert Lewen.*
John Gannett Junior.	*Lawrence Saint Lo.*
William Goldwyer.	*Richard Blackmore.*
Robert Michel.	*Robert Erle.*
John Ridout.	*Daniel King.*
	John Gannett.

Appeal for funds for rebuilding Blandford church. (BM)

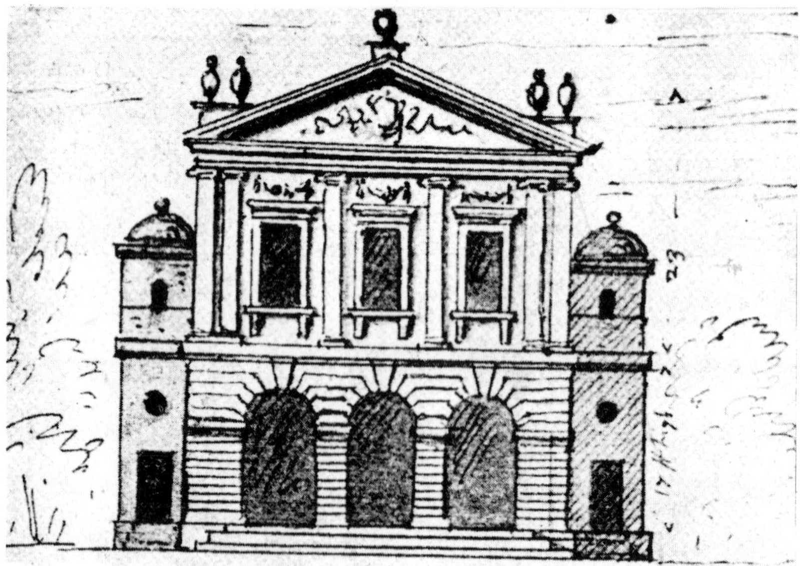

ABOVE: Bastard's House and the fire monument; (SJ) BELOW: Sir James Thornhill's design for the new Town Hall, 1733. (BM)

(19)

THOMAS John & William Bastard

Lost by the Fire that burnt down the Town of Blandford June the 4th. 1731.

All there Stock in Trade, Household and wearing Apparell in the House they lived in which was ye House belonging to Mr Williamses Charoty, on ye South side of ye ... opposet the Church — As by Perticulars in this Book | 25..

All there Stock in Trade, in a Large Barne, & yard Caled the Parsonage Barne, on the noarth side of ye Church Consisting of dry boards, & planks of all Kinds, English & Foreign and Timber in the yard and saw houses, Ladders, a Morning Coach, and a Cart, and finished Work as Sash windows, doors, & Wainscot, Glass, &c, as by Perticulars in this Book | 153..

Corporation 29

Town hall 55-6 by 22-0 is 12 sq. 50	600
old Alms house part flemish walls standing tiled, 12 sq. ½ at 12	150
Skoole house dwelling part 20 square at 18	360
& two Skools with woodhouses and rooms under, old building tiled 13 sq. at 13	169
tiled sheds 2 sq. at 3	6
a Stable thached 2 sq. ¼ at 6	15
a woodhouse thached 4 sq. ½ at 2	8 10

ABOVE: Extract from John Bastard's book showing some of the losses sustained by his family, (DRO) and BELOW: rough estimates of Corporation losses. (DRO)

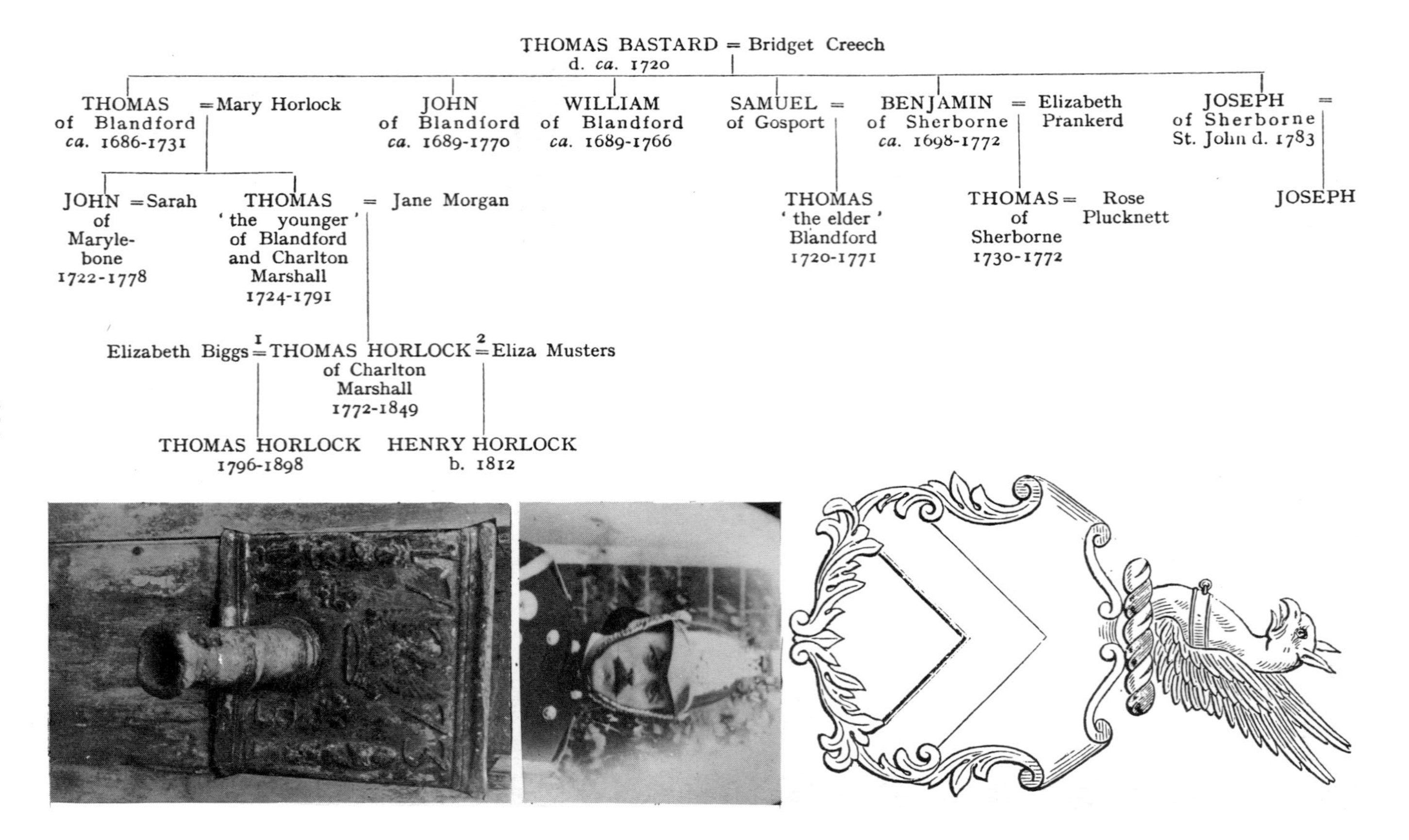
THOMAS BASTARD = Bridget Creech
d. ca. 1720
THOMAS of Blandford ca. 1686-1731 = Mary Horlock
JOHN of Blandford ca. 1689-1770
WILLIAM of Blandford ca. 1689-1766
SAMUEL = of Gosport
BENJAMIN of Sherborne ca. 1698-1772 = Elizabeth Prankerd
JOSEPH of Sherborne St. John d. 1783 =
JOHN of Marylebone 1722-1778 = Sarah
THOMAS 'the younger' of Blandford and Charlton Marshall 1724-1791 = Jane Morgan
THOMAS 'the elder' Blandford 1720-1771
THOMAS of Sherborne 1730-1772 = Rose Plucknett
JOSEPH
Elizabeth Biggs = (1) THOMAS HORLOCK of Charlton Marshall 1772-1849 = (2) Eliza Musters
THOMAS HORLOCK 1796-1898
HENRY HORLOCK b. 1812

A BRIEF

ACCOUNT

OF THE

DREADFUL FIRE

AT

BLANDFORD-FORUM

IN THE

County of DORSET, which happened *June* iv. M.DCC.XXXI.

Together with a

SERMON

Preached at *Blandford, June* 4, 1735. being the Day set apart by the *Protestant Dissenters* there for Prayer and Humiliation under the Remembrance of that SAD PROVIDENCE.

To which is added,

A SERIOUS ADDRESS to the Inhabitants of that Town.

By *MALACHI BLAKE.*

The THIRD EDITION.

Suppose ye that these Galileans *were Sinners above all the* Galileans, *because they suffered such Things? I tell you nay: But except ye repent ye shall all likewise perish.*

Luke xiii. 2, 3.

Rebus angustis animosus atque
Fortis appare : *Hor. Lib.* ii. *Ode* x.
Quantò quisque sibi plura negaverit,
A Diis plura feret. *Hor. Lib.* iii. *Ode* xvi.

This Treatise is not only calculated for the Inhabitants of *Blandford*, but proper for other Families also.

London, *Printed for the* Author, *and sold by* R. Ford, *in the* Poultry; *and* A. Tozer *Bookseller in* Exon. 1736. Price stitch'd One Shilling; Bound One Shilling and Three Pence.

OPPOSITE LEFT: From Bastard family tree; (BM) ABOVE: their arms; (BM) CENTRE: T. Goddard, Blandford's Fire Chief about 1910; (JG) BELOW: pump from rear of Bastards House (note phoenix, and initials J.B.); (BM) ABOVE LEFT: John Bastard; (BM) CENTRE: William Bastard; (BM) RIGHT: title page of Malachi Blake's account of the 1731 fire, (BM) and BELOW: Blandford in flood 1882; note Assembly Room on right. (BMT)

Sans Souci.

The Inhabitants of BLANDFORD and its Vicinity,

ARE RESPECTFULLY INFORMED, THAT

ON SATURDAY AUGUST 24, 1799. AT THE ASSEMBLY ROOM,

Will be performed a new and popular Entertainment, called

The SPHINX.

ARRANGEMENT OF THE RECITATION AND SONGS.

PART I.

Rec. Introduction,
Song. A Laugh at the World,
R. Description of the Sphinx,
Song. The Gardener,

Rec. The Angler,
Song. The Irish Wake,
Rec. The Dasher,
Song. The Lyric Test,

Rec. The Dinner Hunter,
Song. The Nancy,
R. The Cockney out of Town,
S. The Labourer's Welcome Home,

Rec. The Comical Fellow—Song. The Rowdydowdydow.

PART II.

Rec. The Parent,
Song. All's one to Jack,
Rec. Fame,
Song, True Glory,

Rec. Drunken Soliloquy,
S. The Advantage of Toping,
Rec. Wefts and Strays,
Song. The Margate Hoy,

Rec. The Little Colonel,
Song. Captain Wattle and Miss Roe,
Rec. Matrimonial Hints,
Song. The Irish Echo,

Rec. Societies—Song. The Country Club.

PART III.

Recitation. Sir Oliver and the Maiden Speech,
Song. Meg of Wapping,
Rec. The Military Family,
Song. The Soldier's Adieu,

Rec. The Story of Fizgig,
Song. The Italian Music Master,
Rec. Anecdotes,
Song. Nongtongpaw,

Recitation. Exposition of the Sphinx,
Song. Tol de rol de rol,
Rec. Sancho in Barataria,
Song. The Auctioneer.

The whole is written, composed, and will be spoken, sung, and accompanied on an organized Instrument, which has all the Properties of a Band, by

MR. DIBDIN.

Admittance 3s.—Doors to be opened at Seven, and the Performance to begin at Eight o'Clock.

TICKETS sold by Mr. SIMMONDS, Bookseller and Printer, of whom may be had the Songs in all Mr. DIBDIN's Entertainments of SANS SOUCI—The popular Novel of Hannah Hewit—The Younger Brother—A complete history of the Stage, a periodical Work, and every other Article in Mr. DIBDIN's Catalogue.

☞ Mr. DIBDIN respectfully announces that he cannot possibly perform more than ONE Night at BLANDFORD, his Tour being so completely arranged as to employ his whole time till his opening of Sans Souci, in Leicester Place, under the auspices of the LORD CHAMBERLAIN, on the 5th. of October next.

Programme of 1799. (DCM)

Leisure and Pleasure

Fishing, coursing, football, other ball games and cock-fighting were among the spare time activities, of working people, but there was little organised sport before the 19th century. A good deal of time was spent in local hostelries, which were the real social centres. Cottages were tiny and families large and men used the public houses as a place to contact their fellows, to play cards and shove ha'penny, and to get up to date with local news. The women were not expected to attend, and in any event were usually fully occupied with large families. The fairs held in the streets, and later on the Fair Field off Salisbury Road, travelling circuses, menageries and travelling performers provided the occasional diversion.

Bowling and archery were popular in the 16th century. A Borough minute of 1592 reads 'The Play Close was let to Mr Machem then bailiff, at no rent for seven years, he maintaining the same, and to keep all fences in repair during the term. He not to plough or dig up the same, permitting the inhabitants and their friends the use of shooting at the Butt without restraint'. It was important in those days that local men should have facilities for practice in archery. The Borough chamberlain's accounts for the 17th and 18th centuries make frequent reference to the town's two bowling greens and to 'the play field'. The second bowling green was created in 1674 at a cost of £34. In 1699 John Jones was paid £2 17 6d for thatching the bowling green walls.

The story is rather different for the well-to-do of Blandford, of which there were many, who had the benefit of better education, were able to enjoy literature and the arts, hunting, riding, shooting, entertaining and taking holidays.

From 1603 the Blandford Races were held on the Race Down near the present Blandford military camp, and for many years this was the main event of the year, with a large influx of racegoers and owners. For their benefit, wrestling matches, cudgel playing, cock fighting, balls, concerts, dinners and other festivities were arranged. The races continued, with a few breaks, such as during the Commonwealth period when they were banned, until the middle of the 19th century. In 1786 a record was kept of the local gentry attending the races and gives particulars of the carriages in which they arrived:

'Lord Milton, Milton Abbey . . .	Coach and six Bays.
Lord Shaftesbury, St. Giles . . .	Ditto and six Bays.
Lord Arundel, Wardour Castle . .	.Ditto and six Bays.
Mr Sturt, Critchel House	Ditto and six Bays.
Mr Willet, Merley House	Ditto and six Bays.
Mr Weld, Lulworth Castle	Ditto and six Bays.
Mr Portman, Bryanston	Ditto and six Browns.
Mr Drax, Charborough	Ditto and six Piebalds.
Lord Rivers, Rushmore Lodge . .	Coach and four Bays.
Lord DFigby, Sherborne Castle . .	Ditto and four Browns.
Adm[1] Digby, Minterne	Ditto and four Chesnuts.
Mr Rose Drew, Wooton.	Ditto and four Browns.
Rev Mr Richards, Longbridy . . .	Ditto and four Blacks.
Mr Morton Pitt, Kingston	Ditto and four Browns.
Colonel Michel, Dewlish	Ditto and four Blacks.
Mr Blair, Whatcombe	Ditto and four Blacks.
Mr Pleydel, Milborne	Ditto and four Blacks.
Mr Snow, Langton	Ditto and four Browns.
Mr Bower, Iwerne	Ditto and four Bays.
Mr Baker, Ranston	Ditto and four Crop Browns.
Mr Bankes, Kingston Hall	Ditto and four Browns.
Mr Chapman, Gunville.	Ditto and four Browns.
Miss Arundell, Ashcombe	Ditto and four Blacks.
Mr Trenchard, Lytchet.	Ditto and four Crop Browns.
Lady Strafford, Henbury	Ditto and four Bays.
Sir William Hanham, Deans Court .	Phaeton and four Greys.
Mr Fitch, High Hall	Chariot and pair of Bays.
Rev Mr Russell, Gaunts	Ditto and pair of Blacks.
Rev Mr Templeman, Gussage . .	Ditto and pair of Blacks.
Mrs Ridout, Deans Leaze	Ditto and pair of Blacks.
Captain Bingham, Melcombe . .	Ditto and pair of Blacks.
Mr. Pickard, Bloxworth	Ditto and pair of Blacks.
Mr Seymer, Hanford	Ditto and pair of Browns.
Mr Gundry, Rawston	Ditto and pair of Bays.
Mr Beckford, Stepleton	Ditto and pair of Bays.
Mr Jekyll, Spettisbury	Ditto and pair of Browns.
Mr T. Bastard, Blandford	Ditto and pair of Blacks.
Mr J. Bastard, blandford	Ditto and pair of Blacks.
Mr Churchill, Henbury	Ditto and pair of Blacks.
Mr. Elkins, Philliols	Ditto and pair of Blacks.[a]'

The local hunts in the 19th century were the Portman Hounds based at Bryanston, Mr Farquharson's Hounds at Langton Long and the Blackmore Vale.

As early as 1700 Blandford saw itinerant travelling musicians, tumblers and theatre companies staying in the town and often playing in the streets and the public houses. These people were frequently in trouble and often arrested, and removed as vagrants without means of subsistence. Eventually they were able to obtain licences or passes to move from place to place. Theatre companies also had to obtain licences to perform. At the Easter Quarter Sessions in 1789, James Biggs, manager of one of these companies, obtained a licence 'to perform tragedies, comedies, interludes, plays, operas or farces within the borough of Blandford Forum over a period of sixty days.' These travelling theatre companies frequently hired a building such as a barn and adapted it for their purposes — they could be in the town a few days or weeks according to the popularity of the show. Sometimes they erected their own temporary structures on the Marsh or in the Playfield and gave them such names as 'Drury Lane' or 'The Coliseum' for the duration of their stay. Between 1793 and 1812 the Salisbury Theatre Company visited Blandford on many occasions, and leased their own premises in Whitecliff Mill Street which they called the New Theatre. These premises remained in frequent use until offered for sale in 1832 with all the scenery, decorations, lamps etc. The precise location cannot now be pinpointed, but is believed to have been in the general area of Fianders Garage.

The Blandford Assembly Rooms erected in West Street in 1771 were also in frequent use for theatrical performances, musical evenings, language classes, dancing lessons and political meetings. The standard was quite high, particularly in race week, and drew the well-to-do from a wide area. In July 1773, for example, a concert was held at which the composer John Christian Bach, son of Johan Sebastian Bach, was one of the instrumentalists. Tickets on this occasion were seven shillings each.

On 3 July 1752 a cudgel-playing contest was held at the Sword and Dagger, Blandford. Three guineas were offered as prizes – two guineas 'to the man that breaks most heads and saves his own' and one guinea 'to the second best'. Numerous advertisements appeared in the Salisbury papers regarding cock fighting in Blandford. One of 7 July 1755 reads:

'A cock match will be fought at the new cock-pit at Blandford during the time of the races between the gentlemen of Dorset and Wilts. William Rake and William Miles feeders.'

With the improved living conditions, educational advances, and better travel facilities of the mid-19th century, the working classes were gradually able to participate in social activities previously not available to them and were able to improve their own education. Libraries had existed in West Street for many years, the earliest known being those of Samuel Simmonds, a bookseller, from 1764 and William Sollers, son of a former vicar, whose library on the south side of the street was open in 1770.

The Blandford Reading society was formed in March 1792 with 42 members including four clergymen, five lawyers, four surgeons, two gentry, two drapers, a builder, a baker, a grocer and a wine merchant. This existed for the study of literature and for discussions and lectures on a higher plane than that which could be appreciated by the ordinary labouring man. The first public library was opened on 1 January 1833 and was known as the Blandford Commercial Reading Room — this was in the Assembly Rooms and was open from 8am to 9pm. By this time the Assembly Rooms were doubling as a kind of further education centre. William Barnes, the Dorset poet, lectured on numerous occasions at the Blandford Literary and Scientific Institute between 1855 and 1877 on such subjects as 'The Dorset Dialect', 'Ancient Britain', 'The Home and Home Life' and 'The beautiful and good in nature'. He also addressed the Dorset Natural History and Antiquarian Field Club at the Crown Hotel, Blandford, in June 1877 and at the same time inspected Mr H. Durden's collection of local archaeological material (now in the British Museum) and Mr Shipp's collection of fossils (whereabouts not known).

Football had been played in Blandford, as elsewhere, since mediaeval times. The *Salisbury & Winchester Journal* of 2 June 1834 reports Blandford Cricket Club's first meeting 'on the new ground'. In 1883 Blandford played rugby union football against Old Shirburnians at The Fair Field, Blandford.

The agricultural community too had its own organisations. The Farmers Club was formed in 1848 and the Agricultural Society in the following year.

The Blandford Town band also played an important part in the life of the town, turning out at all important events, festivals, balls, civic occasions, weddings and funerals. The composition of the band was varied to meet the occasion. The first known bandmaster was John Barfoot, a member of an old Blandford family, some of whom were engaged in making musical instruments. One of their clarinets, of c1790 can be seen in a a glass case in Shapwick church. He was succeeded by Robert Eyers, who had come to Blandford from Wimborne in 1844 and later became landlord of the Crown hotel. In 1851 he was described as leader of the Blandford quadrille and cornopean bands. He provided music for all occasions and was bandmaster of the Blandford troop of Dorset Yeomanry in 1853 and later of the 8th Dorset (Blandford) Volunteer Rifle Corps. He brought the band to a high standard of excellence and, with the coming of the railways, was able to enter competitions over a wide area. He won a first prize at Exeter in 1861 but the peak of his career was in 1863, when Blandford Town Band won first prize at the Crystal Palace against 21 contestants, comprising the leading bands of the country, to beat the national champions, Dewsbury, into second place. He was succeeded in 1880 by Thomas Hunt.

The 18-hole Ashley Wood golf course, which originally extended to both sides of the Wimborne Road, was opened in 1896 but later, due to traffic problems, was reduced to 9 holes to the north of the road.

A great favourite in Edwardian times was the celebrated Blandford Mouth-organ Band, greatly in demand at concerts and social events held over a wide area.

Although the coming of the railways in the mid-19th century made business and pleasure travel over the whole country much more speedy and comfortable, it made little difference to the lives of the people living here. What did make a good deal of difference was the coming of the bicycle, which offered considerable freedom of movement and, unlike the horse, cost nothing to keep beyond the expense of occasional punctures and repairs, largely due to the state of the roads. While a horse could not reasonably be expected to do more than 20 to 30 miles a day, local 'cycling enthusiasts recorded journeys of from 60 to 100 miles in a day and some 'fisherman's' stories are still told of the enormous mileages claimed by some. It was also good for trade, as persons living in the nearby villages not served by the train could 'cycle in for their shopping, without having to wait in Blandford most of the day to return to their homes by carrier's cart. With the loss of trains and the village 'bus services in recent years the bicycle seems set for a come-back.

Quite a lot of social life went with membership of the many friendly societies operating in the town. They existed mainly to help members in need, but also organised social events and outings for the families. Once a year they had their annual parade or 'club day', marching through the town in full regalia with banners flying.

Blandford's first cinematograph shows, before the first world war, were given at the Fair Field or on the Marsh, by travelling showmen. It is said that when a train hurtled down upon the audience from the screen, they all ducked! There was a permanent cinema in East Street soon after the first world war. This was on the north side and was known as the Picture Palace. The property was subsequently acquired by Mr and Mrs P. J. Carter who, in 1927, carried out improvements and re-opened it as the Palace. It continued there until 1934 when Mr & Mrs Carter had a new cinema built on the opposite side of the road (now Keymarkets). The old Palace was used as a bazaar for a number of years, but the large increase in population at Blandford Camp, and other factors decided Mr & Mrs Carter to re-open the place as a cinema, and it became the Ritz. Often, on Sundays, the same programme was used for both cinemas, the films being rushed across the road at change-over time. The Ritz closed its doors in 1957, as the need for two cinemas had by then diminished, but the Palace continued until it was acquired by Keymarkets. The town now has no cinema at all.

Older residents well remember the travelling players who, until about 1930, used to set up tent near the railway arches at the foot of Damory Street and gave performances – usually blood and thunder melodramas. The shows put on by the Blandford Operatic & Dramatic Society from 1926, including many of Gilbert and Sullivan's operettas and some dramatic productions, are also remembered with pleasure.

Blandford still enjoys a wide range of sporting and cultural amenities for all ages – perhaps the most unusual of these is the Blandford Rural Music School which, since its inception in 1947, has played an important part in the training of young people and adults for musical examinations and scholarships, and to take their places in small groups and orchestras.

The great annual event since 1969 has been the 'Great Working of Steam Engines' which takes place at Stourpaine Bushes each September. It is organised by the Dorset Steam and Historical Vehicles Benevolent Fund. Here people come from all over the country and from abroad to see the showmens' engines, traction, road and fairground engines, fairground organs, oil and petrol-driven vehicles of the past and stationary machinery once familiar on local farms. The working craftsmen, horse ploughing, sheep shearing, cider making and other activities are a great draw. This event, which lasts for three days, has helped to put Blandford on the map, to provide money for deserving charities and to increase the sale of Wellington boots!

Many look back with pleasure to annual shows once put on at the Palace and called 'The Footlight Follies', to the carnival fair held in the main streets and many other activities, including the town band, which seem to be things of the past. The town is, however, fortunate in having on its doorstep the Coade Hall at Bryanston School. The Arts Centre there, erected in the 1960s as a memorial to Thorold Francis Coade, a former headmaster, provides a wide range of musical and dramatic entertainment by orchestras and artistes of high calibre. The Blandford Forum Museum, to be opened in 1984, will provide the town with a long needed amenity and will portray the life, industry and culture of those who have lived hereabouts since pre-historic times.

OPPOSITE ABOVE: Programme of 1828; (DCM) BELOW: Blandford Town Band; National Champions 1863. (BM)

☞Last Night of Performing this Season.

FOR THE BENEFIT OF

Mr. PENSON.

MR. PENSON begs leave to return his most respectful Acknowledgements to the Ladies, Gentlemen, and Public in general, of BLANDFORD and its Vicinity, for the Honour of their Patronage during the Season; and flatters himself that the thorough sense he has of the obligations he owes to this Town, and the Gratitude he feels for them, may encourage him to hope for Continuance of that kind Support it will ever be his study to merit.

BY DESIRE AND UNDER THE PATRONAGE OF

J. J. SMITH Esq.

ON MONDAY EVENING SEPTEMBER, 1st, 1828,
Will be Performed CHERRY'S ADMIRED COMEDY of THE

Soldier's Daughter

Governor Heartall,..Mr. PENSON.—Frank Heartall,..Mr. HARRINGTON.
Mr. Malfort,.....Mr. HARRIS.—Captain Woodley,.....Miss OLD.—Ferret,.....Mr. GROVES.
Timothy Quaint,..Mr. J. PENSON.—Simon,..Mr. JARVIS.—William,..Mr. CLARK.
The Widow Cheerly,.........Miss CROFTON.
Mrs. Malfort,............Mrs. OLD.—Susan,.......Miss CRANMER.
Julia,..................Miss F. OLD.—Mrs. Fidget,......................Mrs HARRIS.

END OF THE COMEDY
The Comic Song of THE COSMETIC DOCTOR,
BY Mr. PENSON.

After which, a New Piece (in one Act) called

PETER SMINK,

Or, WHICH IS THE MILLER?

Peter Smink,..........Mr. J. PENSON.—Chevalier Bayard (disguised as a Miller.)..............Mr. HARRIS.
Hautz (the Miller,)...Mr. PENSON.—The Commandant...Mr. HARRINGTON.
Eugene,........Mr. GROVES.—Peasant,......Mr. JARVIS.
Ninette,..............................Miss OLD.

IN THE COURSE OF THE PIECE WILL BE INTRODUCED THE
Admired Song of I'D BE A BUTTERFLY, BY MISS OLD.
AND THE COMIC SONG OF
"TRUISMS, or INCONTROVERTIBLE FACTS," BY Mr. J. PENSON.

TO CONCLUDE WITH THE FAVOURITE MUSICAL FARCE OF

LOCK AND KEY.

Brummagem,..........................Mr. PENSON.—Captain Vain,.................Mr. HARRIS.
Captain Cheerly,..............Mr. HARRINGTON.—Ralph,.........Mr. J. PENSON.
......Miss OLD.—Selina,......Miss CRANMER.—Dolly,.........Mrs. OLD.—Fanny......Mrs. HARRIS.

TICKETS to be had of Mr. PENSON at the King's Arms, and at the Libraries.

SHIPP, PRINTER, BLANDFORD.

BLANDFORD RACES, 1782.

ON Tuesday, October the 8th. Fifty Pounds will be run for by any Horse, &c. that never won that value at any one time; four-year olds to carry 7 st. 7lb. five-year olds 8st. 7lb. six-year olds 9st. 1lb. aged 9st. 6lb. the best of three four-mile heats.

Mr. Martin's chesnut colt, *Nebuchadnezzar*
4 years old, *Robert Philpot*, striped . . . .
Mr. Helliar's brown colt, *Young Champaign*,
4 years old, Rider unknown . . . .
Mr. Bacon's black Mare, *Florizel*,
5 years old, *Mun. Dilly*, black . . . . . .

☞ Several others expected to enter at the Post.

ON Wednesday, October the 9th. Fifty Pounds, given by the Members for the County; four-year olds, to carry 7st. 7lb. five-year olds, 8st. 7lb. six year olds 9st. 1lb. aged, 9st. 6lb. the best of three four-mile heats. Winners this year to carry 4lb. and of a King's Plate since the 5th. of April, & the winner of the Exeter Cup, 10lb. extra.

Mr. Compton's bay colt. *Cottager*,
4 years old, *Mun. Dilly*, black . . . .
Mr. Helliar's chesnut horse, *Fair Johnny*,
aged, Rider unknown . . .

☞ Several others expected to Enter at the Post.

⁂ To Start each Day at 12 o'Clock.
Assemblies and Ordinaries as usual
An Ordinary for the LADIES at the *Crown-Inn*, where Tickets are to be had for the Assembly.

EVELIN SHIRLEY, Esq. Steward.
JAMES CLARKE, Clerk of the Course.

Printed by S. SIMMONDS, Book-seller, &c. &c.

Blandford Races 1782.

ABOVE: Blandford Mouth-organ Band 1905; (JWN) CENTRE: Portman Hunt grooms about 1910; (BM) BELOW: Blandford Town Band c1912. (BM)

ABOVE: L. B. Bunce's carnival float about 1905; (JG) BELOW: Blandford Market Place illuminations on 300th anniversary of the granting of the Borough charter 1905. Each of the fairy lights consisted of a candle placed inside a small coloured bowl and every one had to be lit by hand! (BM)

ABOVE: Procession through Salisbury Street about 1901, and BELOW: celebrations for the coronation of Edward VII. (BM)

ABOVE: Salisbury Street at the time of Edward VII's coronation; (BM) CENTRE: Cherry's carnival float 1927, (JJH) BELOW: the Footlight Follies, 1962. (JJH)

ABOVE: The first Palace cinema (later re-named the Ritz), (JJH) and BELOW: the new Palace cinema, 1929. (JJH)

ABOVE: The rebuilt Palace (now Keymarkets), (JJH) and BELOW: Hall & Woodhouse's football team known as 'The Tubs', 1929. (JWN)

ABOVE: Blandford Cricket Club about 1920; front left is Alderman B. C. Hunt; (BM) CENTRE: Blandford Cricket Club 1924/25, and (BM) BELOW: Blandford Football Club about 1924.

UNITED F.C.
1931-1932

BF-18

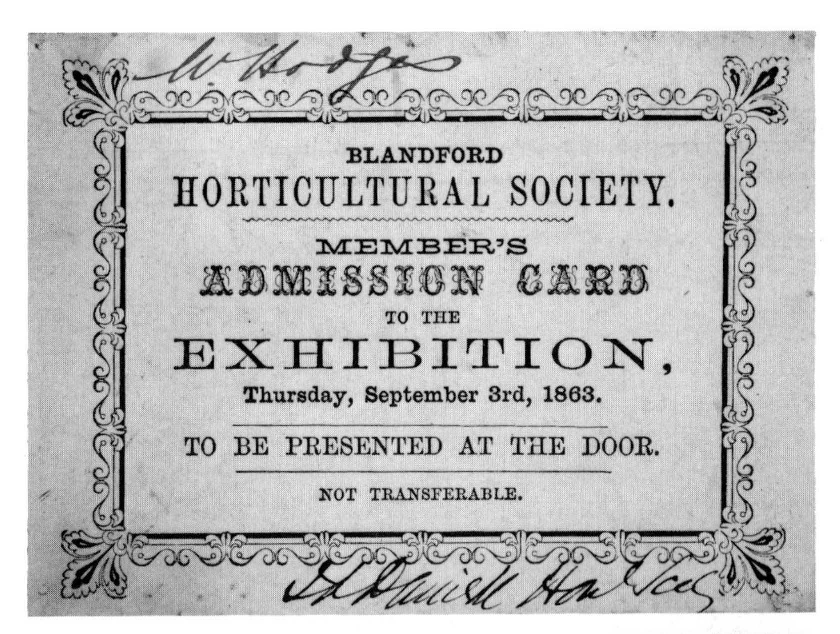

BLANDFORD

HORTICULTURAL SOCIETY.

MEMBER'S

ADMISSION CARD

TO THE

EXHIBITION,

Thursday, September 3rd, 1863.

TO BE PRESENTED AT THE DOOR.

NOT TRANSFERABLE.

OPPOSITE ABOVE: Blandford United Football Club 1931-32; (BM) CENTRE: Mr Conyers' char-a-banc c1921, (JW) and BELOW: An early car in Blandford. (DW) ABOVE: Ticket to Exhibition of Blandford Horticultural Society, 1863; (BM) BELOW: wrestling was a popular diversion at the races. (BM)

CROWN
Family and Commercial Hotel,
AND
GENERAL POSTING ESTABLISHMENT,
BLANDFORD, DORSET.

ROBERT EYERS,
PROPRIETOR,
WINE AND SPIRIT MERCHANT,
Agent for Meux and Co's Stout and Allsopp's and Bass's Ales.

Hunting Gentlemen will find this Establishment replete with every accommodation, being within easy distance of four Packs of Hounds.

Commodious Yard and Excellent Stabling with Loose Boxes,
AND
LOCK UP COACH HOUSES,
Very Superior Stud of Horses, Carriages and Private Omnibuses.
HEARSE AND MOURNING COACHES.

An Omnibus attends the arrival and departure of every train.

Agent by Appointment to the Somerset and Dorset Railway Company.

INLAND REVENUE OFFICE.

Advertisement for the Crown. (BM)

Mind and Spirit

The first church at Blandford was most probably built early in the 12th century, to meet the needs of a developing small town. This church would have been half-timbered on a stone foundation and probably not on the same site as the present parish church. The engraving of the old parish church, destroyed in the great fire of 1731, indicates a 15th century construction with an embattled tower and spire, chancel, nave, two aisles and chapels reserved for the Rogers and Ryves families, who were for many years the principal residents in the town. The Ryves still had substantial interests here in 1731 but the Rogers had sold their estates to Sir William Portman in the 1680s.

The present church was completed between 1732 and 1739 at a cost of £3,200 and opened on 8 April 1739, the work carried out by John and William Bastard. They were no doubt influenced in their design by their association with Thomas Archer, the great baroque architect who created the north front of Chatsworth, and who had employed the Bastards in his building of Chettle House. They had also worked on other country houses in this area under architects and builders favouring this style. Blandford is indeed fortunate in having this baroque gem.

Originally the 1739 church was 120 feet in length with a small apse projecting to the east but with no proper chancel. The roof is supported by ten Ionic pillars of solid Portland stone. The best commentary on the architecture of the church is that contained in Mr Peter Smith's *Blandford*, first published in 1968.

Numerous changes have taken place within the church in recent years, such as the removal of the organ back to its original position and the removal of the side galleries. Quite a remarkable achievement was the movement in 1895, by the use of jacks and rollers, of the apse from its original position to one further east, to provide a new chancel. There are nine bells in the tower, the oldest of which is said to pre-date the 1731 fire and known as 'the apprentice bell'. It was made by William Knight, said to be a Blandford bellfounder, in 1727 and weighs 80 lbs. It was rung each day, morning and evening, to warn apprentices and their masters that it was time to start or finish work — it is said the masters only ever heard the morning bell! For many years this bell lay in the church porch, but it has recently (1976) been rehung.

The old church registers and other parish documents are supposed to have been lost in the 1731 fire but one wonders, for many records, normally kept in the parish chest, and pre-dating the fire, have since been discovered. The church was almost the last place in the town to catch fire and there would have been ample time for the parish chest or its contents to have been removed. A government report of 1834 on the town's charities revealed the existence then of the churchwardens' accounts of 1626.

The churchwardens accounts from 1731, now in the County Record Office, contain some interesting and sometimes amusing entries, such as these few extracted from the 18th century books:

'1736	Paid Nic Upshall for taking care of the boys in the gallery.		3	0d
	55 hedghogs at 2d		9	2d
	1 otter		2	0d
	3 do. sparrow heads		1	6d
	a pole catt			4d'

(there are hundreds of entries in succeeding years for sparrows and other vermin for which extermination payments were payable)

'1737	Paid mending the Tabernackle winders		1	10d
1749	For goose grease for the use of the bells		1	0d
1752	For whipping the pretended dumb fellows and for whipcord (This seems to relate to people trying to get alms by pretending to be dumb)		2	4d
1760	Ringing the bells for King George		18	6d
1761	Ringing the bells for the victory over the French		8	0d
1791	Ringing when there majestys went through town to Weymouth		10	6d
1794	Beer given to the men when the organ was unpacked		5	0d
1795	Richard Kerby for one years salary as organist	20	0	0d
1800	Ringers for Nelson's victory off Copenhagen		10	6d'

In 1542 Dorset was transferred from the diocese of Salisbury to the newly formed diocese of Bristol and remained under Bristol until it was transferred back in 1836. The Archdeacon of Dorset's registry was at Blandford and remained here until 1858. During this period wills came under the jurisdiction of the church courts, where they were proved and grants of probate issued. After 1731 the Archdeacon's and Bishop's courts were held at first 'in the church porch of the late burnt church at Blandford' and later 'at the Red Lyon Inn there'. Many of the Archdeacon's records were lost during the reform riots of the 1830s at Blandford and at Bristol.

In 1735 an episcopal visitation to Blandford Forum brought to the attention of the church court the fact that 'Catherine Piddle, Prudence Paine and Christian Adam have had bastards ... imprudent creatures that do penance yearly without shame'. A typical sentence of penance was to 'stand three market days in the town and three Sabeathe dayes in the church, in a white sheete, with a paper on her back and bosom showing her sinne ...'

Ecclesiastical probate jurisdiction ceased in 1858 when a district registry of the High Court of Justice was established at Blandford, which continued until 1941.

For many years the church had control of premises at the corner of Salisbury Street and Whitecliff Mill Street which, in Victorian times, was known as the Corner Coffee House or the Church House. It was a sort of welfare centre and offered various services. The parish nurse attended, baths could be obtained and classes were held for boys to learn handicrafts.

Henry VIII's break with the Church of Rome, the reasons for which were well enough known in the town by the ordinary person, led to a general discontent with his newly established Church of England. The Conventical Act of 1593 made secret religious meetings of dissenters and Catholic recusants illegal and those found meeting were severely punished. Poor people went to the established church because they had to by law and, after 1601, because they often needed the financial help provided by the overseers of the poor administered by the Vestry.

In 1650 Rev William Alleine was appointed rector of Blandford Forum in place of Rev John Lindsay, who had been sequestered by Parliament and deprived of his living due to his loyalty to the King. Following the restoration of the monarchy in 1660, William Alleine was not prepared to comply with the provisions of the Act of Uniformity which followed, resigned his living and, with a considerable following, formed the first congregation of protestant dissenters in Blandford, becoming their minister. John Lindsay was then restored to his living. His son, Thomas, who was born at Blandford, became Archbishop of Armagh.

In 1672 Charles II issued a Declaration of Indulgence repealling the penal laws against non-conformists. Although this was a short lived reprieve, in that year meetings were held at Blandford in the house of John Paige, a grocer. He issued a trade token, bearing the arms of the Grocers Company, in 1664.

The Toleration Act of 1689 restored the right of dissenters to hold meetings and the following licences were issued by Dorset Quarter Sessions for Presbyterian meetings in the private houses of:

'1705 John Nichols, Clothier. Blandford
1717 Elizabeth Perkins, Blandford
1721 William Jacobs, Blandford
1722 Matilda Blake, Blandford'

In 1692 the congregation worshipped in Langhorne's barn, which was between upper Salisbury Street and Whitecliff Hill Street. A new meeting house was built in 1722, which was 'set apart for the worship of Almighty God by the people of Christ, called Presbyterians'. A licence was granted by Quarter Sessions in 1733 for services to be held in the new meeting house erected to replace the 1722 chapel destroyed in the 1731 fire. The 1832 chapel was replaced in 1867 by the present building to which additions have subsequently been made.

Some of the ministers of this church remained in office for long periods. Malachi Blake was there from 1716 to 1760, Henry Field from 1760 to 1819, Richard Keynes from 1821 to 1853, Benjamin Gray from 1855 to 1890 and Gomer Evans from 1906 to 1924.

Rev John Angel James, who was born in Blandford in 1785, grew up in the town during Henry Field's ministry. He became minister of the famous Carrs Lane meeting house in Birmingham, where he was held in great esteem and where he served the whole of his ministry of 54 years. The John Angel James Memorial buildings were added in his honour in 1904. Mr Malachi Fisher, a prominent Blandford merchant involved in the button-making industry, was the first dissenter to be elected to the Borough Council after the passing of the 1834 Municipal Corporations Act. He became Mayor of Blandford in 1840. He had been superintendent of the Sunday School for 60 years.

The Wesleyan Methodists were active in Blandford during the time of John Wesley's ministry. The earliest known reference to them is in the diary of George Storey, an itinerant preacher of the Salisbury circuit of 1784/5. He refers to being in Blandford with the Methodist community and buying a hymn book from George Higton of Blandford, who he described as living 'near the Wool Pack, Top of Salisbury Street'. In April 1789 a licence was issued to John Twentyman of Doctors Close, Blandford, to hold meetings in his house. The Blandford members in 1795, in addition to John Twentyman, were:

John Harding; Ann Harding; John Rolls; Elizabeth Godwin; Fran. Herman; Sarah Oliver; Ann Twentyman; Mart. Popler; Catherine Mahone; Elizabeth Nickols; Sarah Rolls; William Freeman; Ben. Baverstock; Charles Baverstock; George Gale; Mary Stickland; Maria Oxford; Elizabeth Kail; Mary Hiscock; A. M. Baverstock; Thomas Ryall; Rachel Hill; William Ryall; Mary Gale; Mary Popler.

Although membership was down to 10 by 1805, a revival was on the way as, by 1833, they acquired a site for a purpose-built chapel in Doctors Close. Their first chapel was built on this land in 1834.

The present chapel, incorporating the original to its east, was built in 1874, and included school rooms. Further school rooms, on land given by Mr A. C. Woodhouse, were added to the west in 1905.

The Primitive Methodists formed their separate community in the middle of the 19th century, and erected their chapel in Albert Street in 1877, adding a Sunday School in 1894. The Primitive Methodists were united with the Wesleyans in 1932, but the two communities continued to attend their separate chapels until 1976, after which date all Methodist services have been held at the Close.

The Albert Street chapel was made available in October 1977 for services of the congregation of the Blandford Evangelical church. From January 1973 the Evangelical church meetings had met at Lower Bryanston Farm.

There is not much evidence for any community of the Society of Friends (Quakers) in Blandford. A licence was granted in October 1706 for meetings to be held by them at the house of Thomas Carter, and another granted in July 1742 was for meetings in the house of Elizabeth Garde.

In the 1860s the 'Open' Brethren were meeting in Blandford, mostly in private houses, but sometimes at the 'Iron Room' in Alexandra Street or at the assembly rooms in West Street. By the 1880s they had a sufficiently large following to the able to erect their own meeting place in East Street, which became known as the East Street Hall. Due to a decline in support they were obliged to give up this building, which then became the Labour Hall and is now an art gallery.

On Henry VIII's break with the Church of Rome the Catholics, who had always occupied the parish church, were forced underground, and those caught attending or conducting services were subjected to severe punishments. In 1581 the Blessed Eustace White, a Roman Catholic priest, was arrested in Blandford, tortured and eventually hanged at Tyburn. A revival, or coming out into the open, occurred in Blandford towards the end of the 18th century, when greater tolerance was shown to dissenters. On 21 April 1794 a licence was granted by Quarter Sessions for worship by Roman Cathlics in a chapel at Blandford. Pigot's Directory of 1842 confirms that a chapel was being used by them at Blandford, but its location is at present uncertain. Later in the 19th century they were known to be attending mass at Spetisbury Priory. After this property was sold for secular use in 1927, the mass was celebrated in the private house of Miss Blundell at Blandford St Mary and at the Old House in the Close in Blandford. The present church of Our Lady of Lourdes and St Cecilia, in Whitecliff Mill Street, was built in 1934.

From the 19th century the churches and chapels of the town did much to improve the education and social life of the working classes. They provided mid-week activity with talks on a variety of subjects, adult education classes, debates and discussions and musical evenings. There were two or three 'coffee taverns' opened at different times and places in the town where 'the devil in the glass' was not present. It was at chapel or church that many chose to meet their friends and have their social life. The only other choices were to stay at home or visit the public houses; the public seemed to be divided on these alternatives and after church-going ceased to be compulsory, about one third of the men and two thirds of the women, young people and children attended church or chapel.

Before school attendance was made compulsory in 1880, primary education for the poor was only available at Sunday Schools or in charity schools. It is fair to say that the dissenting chapels did a great deal more towards teaching their children to read, write and add up than did the established church.

The town has a fine record as regards the provision of educational facilities from mediaeval times to the present day. The first school of which we have records was the mediaeval grammar school, owned by the Borough of Blandford Forum, which managed it from funds provided by charities and from fees collected from parents. It retained its mediaeval title of 'the free grammar school in Blandford Forum' long after admission could only be obtained on payment. Details of the original foundation cannot now be ascertained, but a record survives confirming that the school was re-built in the sixth year of the reign of Elizabeth I (1563/4). Another record, of 1579, described the school as being 'of great fame'. The school catered primarily for the sons of the well-to-do in Dorset and adjoining counties, who were boarded in the school house. Among those who had their early education there were William Wake (1657-1736), who became Archbishop of Canterbury, and John Aubrey (1626-1697), the distinguished historian and biographer, who described the school as 'the most eminent school for the education of gentlemen in the west of England'. After the fire of 1731 the school was again rebuilt, on a site north-west of the church, now identified as the Old Bank House. The Borough sold the school premises in 1841 to the schoolmaster, who opened a Savings Bank there in addition to taking pupils on a private basis. The proceeds of sale were used to pay for a 'new market hall' behind the town hall which was subsequently replaced by the present Corn Exchange.

Archbishop William Wake, referred to above, who had 13 children of his own, provided in his will for the financing of a trust for the education of poor boys of Blandford. He died in 1736, but the scheme did not come into operation until 1757. The trust funds were managed bythe Borough Council. The scheme did not provide for the erection of a separate school building for the boys, who had to be educated in the homes of self-employed school masters. The masters were paid £1 a year for each boy. The trustees clothed the boys in the style of the London charity schools. The uniform was varied from time to time but for most of its existence consisted of a dark blue gown, breeches, yellow or orange stockings and white neck-tabs, and they became known as 'the blue-coat boys'. It is unfortunate that not one set of uniform can be traced. After 1831 the boys were taught in the National schools in Park Road with the other town children.

At a meeting of the Town Council on 10 May 1939 it was resolved that no further boys be appointed to the school and the trust was wound up in 1940, largely because parents no longer wished their children identified as 'charity boys', and the boys themselves were reluctant to wear the uniform. The last few to be admitted were George Lowe (1928), Victor Moors (1928), Harry Whitlock (1928), Leonard Hall (1929), Frank Hall (1929), Ronald Fluck (1929), Walter Clark (1930), Ralph Cox (1930), Percy Matthews (1930), Reginald Riggs (1931), Bertie Andrews (1931), Douglas Ellis (1931), John Matthews (1932), Leslie Pike (1932), George Andrews (1932), William James Pike (1933), Eric James Rideout (1933), Reuben Clark (1933), Derek Dodds (1934), Arthur Henry Clarke (1935), Frederick Portsmouth (1935), Kenneth March (1935), Bertie George Pike (1936), Arthur James Freak (1936), Leslie Donald Bellows (1936), Thomas John Freak (1936), William Pike (1936), Eric Smith (1936), Peter Gibbs (1937), David Gibbs (1937), and James Clark (1937).

For nearly 60 years Blandford had another grammar school – the Milton Abbey Grammar School, the original foundation of which dates back to the time of William Middleton, Abbot of Milton Abbey (1483-1525). In 1784 Lord Milton, Earl of Dorchester, the owner of the Milton Abbas estate, obtained an act of Parliament which resulted in the school being moved into Blandford to premises in East Street which he provided. Soon after its removal the school accommodated something like 100 boys and was held in high esteem, often being referred to as 'The Eton of the West'. One of the last pupils of the old school was Thomas Masterman Hardy, one of Nelson's captains at Trafalgar. Rev John Hutchins, the Dorset historian, was for a time a master there. The success of this school, which was run by independent trustees, was one of the reasons why the Borough Council of 1841 decided to close its own grammar school. The following distinguished persons were recorded in 1907 as having had their schooling at Milton Abbey grammar school: Philip Henry Gosse, the great naturalist, Bishop Smythies, the missionary Bishop of Central Africa, General Lord Grenfell, commanding the forces in Ireland, Judges Handley, Clarence and Roe, Admiral Churchill, Sir Robert K. Douglas of the British Museum, R. Bosworth Smith the Dorset naturalist and author, Sir Charles Pennington CB, and Colonel Hastings.

The school continued to function in the town, with various ups and downs, and periods when it was closed altogether, until 1927, when the trustees decided to move it to Whatcombe Manor, some three miles out of Blandford. This proved a disastrous decision and it closed down entirely in 1929.

The Blandford Secondary school was founded in 1862, originally for girls only, by Thomas Horlock Bastard of Charlton Marshall. It was at first called the Milldown Endowed School and, as insufficient numbers of girls were entered, became a mixed school. The premises were on the west side of Damory Street and, following the closure of the Milton Abbey Grammar School, became known as Blandford Grammar School. It achieved considerable academic success until it closed in 1968 on being moved to new premises on Bryanston deer-park, where it was made 'comprehensive' and renamed the Blandford Upper School.

There were few opportunities for education of the poor, other than those provided by the church and chapels, until early in the 19th century. The National Schools movement, founded by the Church of England in 1811, sponsored the first National School in Blandford. This is shown on Thomas Pryde's survey map of 1822 as having been erected in Damory Street in 1821. This later became the girls and infants' elementary school and is now converted into private residences. Larger National schools were subsequently built in Park Road which, with numerous additions, are now called the Archbishop Wake First School.

In 1808 followers of Joseph Lancaster, a Quaker, formed the Royal Lancastrian Society, to carry out his educational ideas for the children of the working classes other than those wishing to attend the Church of England's National schools. There was a school building called the Lancastrian Free school in Salisbury Street, mentioned in 1815 as being 'opposite Williams' drapery warehouse'. The Society subsequently became known as the British & Foreign School Society. A directory of 1848 shows a 'British school' in Whitecliff Mill Street catering for about 100 children drawing support mainly from non-conformist families. Some of its records can be seen at the Dorset County Record Office.

In 1889 the Bryanston Street Mission Room, provided by the Portman family, was taking as many as 89 children to Sunday School. This is probably the 'ragged school' referred to in local directories of the time as being in Bryanston Street.

For those who could pay, there were numerous 'Dame' and private schools taking small numbers of private pupils. Among these were the Misses Hillary & Johnson's establishment for young ladies (1865); the Misses Barter's establishment for young ladies, Cliff View House (1865); Mrs Mary Jane Edwards, Market Place, Professor of music, drawing and French (1868); Miss Isabella Hill's private day school in the Market place (1865); Mrs Roe's boarding school in Salisbury Street (1866); Jane Hillyers's private school, East Street (1851) and the Blandford Academy in Salisbury Street (1865).

A somewhat larger private school, established in Salisbury Street in the 19th century, was St Christopher's and was for girls only. This was later amalgamated with St Leonard's Preparatory School for boys and girls, which functioned until quite recent years. The site is now Fisher's Close and quite near to the modern St Leonard's Middle School.

Within easy reach of the town is Bryanston School, a public school opened in 1927 in the former mansion of the Portman family, with nearby Knighton House a preparatory boarding school for girls. Clayesmore School at Iwerne Minster is another public school and Croft House at Shillingstone, which prepares girls for the professions and universities, also enjoys public school status.

The modern town schools are Archbishop Wake's First School in Park Road, the Milldown First School, The Milldown Middle School, the St Leonards Middle School and the Upper School.

For its size, Blandford can be proud of the many who have distinguished themselves in life, following their birth and/or early education at Blandford, including:

1566 Rev Thomas Bastard, poet. (DNB)
1875 Rev Henry Joy Fynes-Clinton, author. (WWW, d.1959)
1659 Thomas Creech, poet & tralsnator. (DNB)
1792 Rev William Dansey, author. (DNB)
1687 Rev Richard Derby, religious author.
1757 Rev William England, religious author.
1865 Sir Alfred Downing Fripp, surgeon. (WWW, d.1930)
1770 John Kingston Galpine, botanist. (DNB)
1862 Benjamin Kirkman Gray, writer on sociology. (DNB)
1865 George Buchanan Gray, religious author. (DNB)
1821 Rev Arthur Malortie Hoare, religious author. (Boase)
1820 Rev George Tooker Hoare, miscellaneous author. (Boase)
1885 Eric Robert James Hussey, administrator. (WWW, d.1958)
1785 Rev John Angell James, author. (DNB & Boase)
1789 Rev Thomas James, nonconformist minister & author
1656 Rev Thomas Lindesay, Archbishop of Armagh. (DNB)
1683 Rev Samual Lisle, Bishop of Norwich. (DNB)
1876 James Cole Marshall, surgeon. (WWW, d.1952)
1699 Christopher Pitt, poet. (DNB)
1706 Henry Pitt, poet.
1653 Robert Pitt, surgeon, author. (DNB)
1841 Sir Charles Arthur Roe, legal author. (WWW, d.1927)
1583 Sir Thomas Ryves, author. (DNB)
1601 Rev William Sherley, religious author. (Hutchins)
1809 William Shipp, local history author.
1904 Edward Tenney Casswell Spooner, bacteriologist. (WW)
1809 William Charles Spooner, vet & author. (DNB & Boase)
1855 Morton Grey Stuart, 17th Earl of Moray, archaeologist (WWW, d.1930)

1657 Rev William Wake, Archbishop of Canterbury. (DNB)
1825 Caroline Watts, blind poetess.
1898 Pte. Jack (Thomas) Counter. Victoria Cross.
1866 Brig-General Frederick Francis Daniell. (WWW, d.1937)
1834 General Francis Edward Halliday. (WWW, d.1911)
1800 Major General Sir George Moyle Sherer. (Boase)
1818 Alfred Stevens, painter, sculptor. (DNB)
c.1890 Helen Margaret George, painter, sculptor. (Bénézit)

(WW='Who's Who'. WWW='Who Was Who' Boase='Modern English Biography' DNB=Dictionary of National Biography)

APPENDIX V

TEXT OF MANUSCRIPT NOTE IN BODLEIAN LIBRARY WRITTEN c1677 by CHRISTOPHER WASE.

'BLANDFORD FORUM in the County of Dorsett (parcel of the Ducy of Lancaster) hath antiently beene a schoole of good repute. In the vj. of Elizabeth (1563/4) the cheefe inhabitants at a meeting then held made an agreement, and did amongst them enlarge the schoole and did build a convenient and good house for the schoole and did build a convenient and good house for the school-master to receive and borde tablers (=boarders) in which are roomes sufficient to take 60 or 70 tablers and a family (=household) sufficient for their entertainment. In it is a court for the tablers to play in and a garden convenient for the house, the land of which house backside and garden is conveyed by John Pitt of Blandford and his two two sonnes William Pitt and John Pitt unto Trustees and their heires for ever, to be lett at modderate rates to such a schoolmaster as shall be authorised by the Bayliffe and Constabells of the sayd Burrough for the time beeing, and such other inhabitants as have borne office of Bayliffe and not to be converted to any other use whatsoever. And the rent the schoolmaster pays is 26s 8d per annum.

TO the schoolmaster is given by one Mr Williams deceased £5 per annum for the teaching of 2 poore men's sonnes and they pay 4d per quarter only.

THE Bayliffe and burgesses give the schoolmaster for his better encouragement £20 per annum. And at his entrance they give him a lease for his life, and cont (. . .) to pay him such a sallery. Every towne borne child pays 5s per quarter and quarterly 6d for the ringing of the bell and 2s 6d entrance. Every stranger pays 10s per quarter 6d for ringing of the bell, and 5s entrance. AND boath towne borne and strangers pay at Michaelmas 1s 6d for fier and candell, and presents at Newyearstide.

The Schoolmaster when this house was built was one Mr Miller since him Mr Rooke, Mr Gardner, Mr Eaton, Mr Sutto n, Mr

Barstall, Mr Warren, Mr Tidcum, Mr Stephens, Mr Thacum, Mr Carman, Mr Welsteede, Mr Trussell and the present incumbent is Mr Curgannon.

The schoolmaster is obliged to teach after Winchester way, and in all things to follow their customs.'

APPENDIX VI

LIST OF INCUMBENTS

The incumbency was originally in the gift of the Dean and Chapter of Winchester, but was transferred to the gift of the Lord Bishop of Salisbury. In 1853 the Rectory and Vicarage were consolidated by the Patrons for the improvement of the incumbency.

1295 Henry de May
1305 William de Wymborn Holt
1306 John Corneys
1311 William Notelle
1312 William de Marisco
1316 Ralph de Ponte
Canon William de Ayston
1337 Thomas Hare
John Haytfield
1377 Thomas Dennet or Druet
1405 John Besslys
1423 William Bryt
1423 John Brytt
1424 Waelter Hyder
1425 Chaplain John Rouvyle or Rowyle
John Hawlyn
1446 John Skyttish, alias Portland
1467 William Crampesly
1490 Richard Lancaster
William Cressatt
1521 Canon Thomas Claughton
1554 Henry Willies
1558 Hugh Bagwell
1573 Alexander Clevely
1580 George Hansom
1592 William Arnold
1615 John Driver
1639 John Lindesey
1653 William Allen (Intruder)
1666 John Lindesey
1680 John Herne
1681 Richard Roderick
1701 Tho. Sutton
1712 Tho. Rley, M.A.
1736 Thomas Sollers, M.A.
Ven. Archdeacon Samuel Rolleston, M.A.
1776 (Died). John Cooth, M.A.
1776 Chaplain Samuel Nott, M.A.
1793 Canon Joseph Garnett
1800 Joseph Godfrey Sherer, B.A.
1807 Ven. Archdeacon Charles James Hoare, M.A.
1821 George Wm. John Chard, M.A.
1836 Humphrey Simmen Parker, M.A.
1853 William Harte, B.A.
1869 James Richard Quirk, M.A.
1877 Charles Henry Fynes-Clinton, M.A.
1913 Raymond Alured Bond, M.A.
1916 Francis Edward Overton, M.A.
1924 Fredk. Wm. Thmpson Greenwood, D.D.
1929 Harold Oldfield Parnell, M.A.
1935 Charles Frank Hall, O.B.E.
1943 Bertram Thomas Rosson, M.A.
1959 Herbert Godfrey Goodall, M.A.
1972 Richard Andrew Babington, M.A.

Blandford old church. (BM)

John & William Bastard's original plan for the new parish church, 1731, (DRO) and INSET: John Angell James. (BM)

Interior of parish church before removal of apse to a position further east. (SJ)

ABOVE: East end of parish church showing the extended chancel area and position of organ before its removal to west end, (SJ) and BELOW: the Parish Church c1850. (BM)

BLANDFORD.

SEIZURE

FOR

CHURCH RATES.

The Churchwardens of this Parish, Mr. W. T. Elgar and Mr. Robert Lock, in the exercise of the *Legal Authority* which they possess to *compel* those who dissent from the CHURCH OF ENGLAND, to contribute towards the support of its worship, have caused to be seized

TWO CARTS,

from Mr. H. F. FISHER, in payment of £4. 2. 10, the amount of RATE demanded.

The Carts were disposed of in the Market Place, by Mr. Clarke, of Wimborne — the Auctioneers of this Town refusing to co-operate in such an unpopular undertaking. The amount realized was £5. 2. 6, the real value of the property being about £10.

It is unnecessary to comment on the *unscriptural character of the above proceedings.*

April 27th. 1859.

BARTLETT, PRINTER, BOOKSELLER, &C., BLANDFORD.

ABOVE: Dissenters strongly objected to paying church rates; (DCM) OPPOSITE: minutes of sittings and appointment of book-keepers, Presbyterian church, 1732. (BM)

March 16:= 1732:

We the Minister Subscribers & Members of this Church and Congregation of Protestant Dissenters in Blandford forum in the County of Dorset Being met together and having publickly read and duely Considered the following Rules Relating to the Seats and Sittings in our Meeting house Inserted in this Book, Agree that these Shall be deemed as Standing Rules to be observed by us, nor Shall any alterations be made in them or Additions made to them unless with the approbation and Consent of a Majority of us publickly Sumoned together for that purpose. In Testimony whereof the Major part of us, In behalf of our Selves, and others present, Subscribe our names

---

And — We agree to Chuse Mr John Clench and Mr John Frampton Bookeepers for the Ensuing year —

Malachi Blake.
Rt Brooke
Jn: fframpton
John Clench
Nath Bonifield
James Greenway
Richd Clench
George Michell
Ambrose Riles
Jos Lockyer
William Scaper
Thomas Lacy
Wm Haines
John Moore

Willm Watten
Henry Seller
Abraham Meare
Edward Seller
William Parker
Jacob Turner
John Evans

Presbyterian Chapel

LEFT: The original Wesleyan Methodist chapel of 1834; (BM) RIGHT: John Aubrey, 1626-1697; BELOW: Roman Catholic church of Our Lady of Lourdes and St Cecilia. (BM)

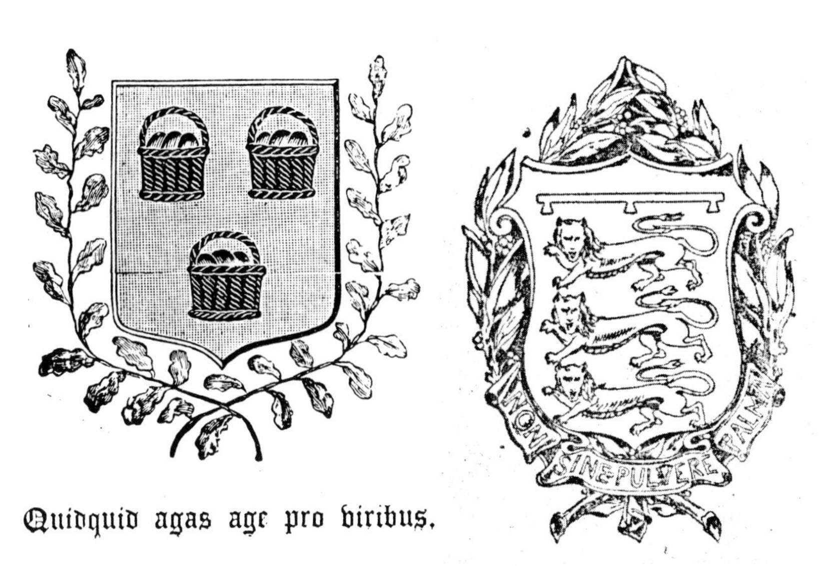
Quidquid agas age pro viribus.
NON SINE PULVERE PALMA

Received Octr. 19th 1772 of
Mr. Jn. Smith Bailiff the sum
of Twelve Pounds in full for
the late Lord Arch Bishop
Wakes Charity Boys one Years
Schooling due, at Midsummer
Last past ℔ me
Matt: Harding
£ 12 " 0 " 0

LEFT: Milton Abbey Grammar School badge; (BM) RIGHT: Blandford Grammar School badge, (BM) and BELOW: receipt by first Master of the Blue-coat school for his salary, 1772. (DRO)

Borough of Blandford Forum } At a Comon Council held in
in the County of Dorset ——— } the Guildhall in and for the
said Borough, on the 31st day of
August in the year of Our Lord 1757
before William Bastard Gentleman, Bailiff, and the
Capital Burgesses whose names are subscribed hereto
it is agreed that the front House called the Schoolhouse
& the necessary House thereto belonging be put in Tenantable
repair forthwith; and the Room called the School Room be
floor'd plaister'd and glazed, and a good strong ledged
Door with a Shed over the same be put thereto, also that
half the said Room be desked in a plain manner, with
Benches round the same, likewise that the two Rooms over
the said School Room be floor'd with Elm, plaister'd and
glazed, and that the above work be done by Messrs John
and William Bastard.

Willm Bastard Bailiff
John Bastard
Thos Fitzherbert
Thos Waters
John White

ABOVE: Minute of Borough Council concerning repairs to the school, 1757; (DRO) BELOW: Blandford Grammar School (formerly Blandford Secondary School). (BM)

LEFT: William Wake, Archbishop of Canterbury; (BM) RIGHT: Alfred Stevens (1817-1875) sculptor, painter and designer, born at Blandford; (BM) BELOW: Form IV, Blandford Secondary School 1915-16. (BM)

ABOVE: United Reform Church, Salisbury Street (formerly Congregational) built 1867, (JG) and BELOW: Blandford Grammar School speech day, November 1962. (SJ)

Blue-coat boy with pet c1920. (SJ)

This is to acquaint any Gentleman who may have Occaſion,

THAT JOHN SPINNEY, Clock and Watch-Maker, at Blandford, in the County of Dorſet, has an exceeding good Church or Turret Clock now made, and alſo an Eight-Day one in Hand, that will be finiſhed ſoon.

Whoever may have an Occaſion for ſuch, any other Sort of Clocks, ſhall have them on very reaſonable Terms, and (if required) twelve Months Trial for Proof.——He is to be ſpoke with at Woodbury-Hill and Shroton Fairs, and ſells all Sorts of Silver, Braſs, Ironmonger's, and Cutlers Goods, at the loweſt Prices; and gives the beſt Prices for all Sorts of old Metal.——Whoever will favour him with their Orders, will greatly oblige

Their humble Servant,

JOHN SPINNEY.

SCARCITY OF CHANGE.

Shopkeepers, Tradesmen, and the Public in general, are respectfully informed, that they may be supplied with

Silver Tokens,

Value ONE SHILLING each,

as an accomodation during the present scarcity of Coin, and that a Bank Note of One Pound will be given in exchange for Twenty of such Tokens, upon application to

HENRY WARD.

Blandford, Sept. 25, 1811.

SIMMONDS, PRINTER, BLANDFORD.

ABOVE: One of Blandford's earliest book-sellers, c1770; (BM) CENTRE: advertisement by John Spinney, 1763; (BM) BELOW: Henry Ward was a well known watch and clock maker and inventor of scientific instruments. (DCM)

Gainful Employment

From its emergence as a town in early mediaeval times until recent years the economy of Blandford Forum has been primarily dependent upon farming. The main crops on the chalk downlands were wheat and barley, and these were dependent on the folding of vast flocks of sheep. Until about 150 years ago the town was almost entirely self-supporting, with every kind of trade carried on to provide its basic needs. One of the main concerns of town leaders was to maintain the high reputation of its great sheep, wool, cheese and cattle markets and fairs, and as a commercial centre. The Borough depended upon tolls for its main income and an on-the-spot market was available for the many local traders and craftsmen. The whole system was carefully monitored, originally by the Court Leet, and later by the Borough Council. Goods could only be sold in the Market Place on market days and persons endeavouring to set up shop outside the official markets or fairs, with the object of avoiding tolls, were dealt with severely. By the 18th century the town provided additional employment in the brewing, tanning, boot and shoemaking, wig making and wheelwrighting trades. People came to Blandford for their clothes, medical supplies and treatment, to bank, to see their lawyers and to meet their friends. Some of the smaller industries of the 18th century included watch and clock making, candle and soap making, saddlery and straw-bonnet making.

One often reads that Blandford had a flourishing glass-painting industry in the 17th century. John Aubrey, the famous antiquary and historian, who spent part of his school days at Blandford in the 1630s, visited 'old Harding, the only country glass painter that ever I knew'. It would seem, however, that this was a one-family business rather than a general industry. In 1659 the Borough chamberlain paid Mathew Harding £1 3 9d for glazing the guildhall windows. It seems likely that 'old Harding,' was Richard Harding, an artist of some considerable talent, and not only involved in glass painting. *The Chronicle of Cranborne* written by Dr Carnegie, and printed by Shipp of Blandford in 1841, includes a map, drawn in 1618, by Richard Harding of Blandford, showing the bounds of the Chase. Old Blandford church probably contained some of his work, as

Richard Symonds' notes on his visit to the church in 1644 refer to the windows having been 'lately done in painted colours'. The Hardings were still involved with glass a hundred years later as, in 1723, John Harding was paid 'for glazing the new window in the jaylehouse'. He also appears in the list of persons living on the east side of Salisbury Street who suffered loss in the fire of 1731.

Another cottage industry of the 17th century was that of band-string making. These were for securing bands worn round the neck and made either of ribbon with bows and ends hanging down in front, or of a silk cord with tassels. Their fame gave rise to the saying 'as strong as a Blandford band-string'. They were popularised by James I, who used one to keep his ruff in place. At the peak of the band-string era the principal merchant organising work here was William Ware. A trade token issued by him in 1668 has a representation of a band string upon it. They went out of fashion in the 1770s, but this was not a major disaster for Blandford operatives, who were quickly absorbed into other cottage industries – stocking and glove knitting and, later, button making.

Daniel Defoe came to Blandford in the early 18th century and in his *Tour through the whole of Britain* published in 1724, describes Blandford lace as the finest in England, and that he was shown some 'so exquisitely fine as I think I never saw better in Flanders, France or Italy'. The skill was handed on from mother to daughter and there are still many expert ladies in the Blandford area.

Blandford was never one of the principal cloth-making towns of Dorset in spite of the multitudes of sheep bred on the downs around it, but the industry was carried on here in the 17th and 18th century and probably continued until the early part of the 19th century. The records of the Sun Fire Office, now preserved in the Guildhall Library, show that there were still numerous associated trades still here after the 1731, fire which must have destroyed most buildings and stock-in-trade. The traders taking out policies with that office were: 1727 John Frampton, Woolstapler; 1730 Jacob Turner, Clothier; 1731 Ambrose Wheeler, Dyer; 1733 Nathaniel Banjafield, Woolstapler; 1741 Robert Frampton, Dyer; 1743 Thomas Benjafield, Woolstapler; 1754 Samuel Scutt, Hosier; 1762 William Nichols, Woolstapler.

Blandford was known in the 18th and 19th centuries for its clock makers. Probably the most famous of these was Henry Ward, who reached his zenith early in the 19th century. He was an inventive person, devised several improvements to clock mechanisms and received several awards, including a Soceity of Arts medal for an improvement to the signal semaphore operated from Telegraph Hill on Blandford Racedown. This signal station was one of a chain in southern England erected on high ground for use during the

Napoleonic wars and until 1837, when the elect telegraph come into use. In 1811 he struck two varieties of silver shillings for local circulation as tokens.

The Mew, Pegler, Spinney, Bennett, Hood and Wyatt families were among the many engaged in this trade. Several of them were also gunsmiths. A fine early 18th century long-case clock by Joseph Mew of Blandford can be seen in Dorchester Museum.

Blandford's largest industry in the 18th and 19th centuries, outside agriculture was the making of buttons. The industry was started in Shaftesbury by Abraham Case in the 1620s. During the following century the Case family opened depôts throughout East Dorset. Most of the buttons were made by women and children working in their own homes. Agents made regular visits to distribute materials and collect finished work. These were sold all over the country and exported to Canada, America, Australia and the continent of Europe. The original 'High Top' buttons were made from a disc of sheep's horn covered with linen on which a wax-thread pattern was worked. The district's extensive sheep farming ensured no shortage of supplies until reels of wire from Birmingham started to arrive. The children doing the preparatory work of making rings from this wire had to twist and solder them and string them into one-gross bundles. They were known as 'winders', 'dippers' and 'stringers'.

In Blandford, Robert Fisher opened a button depôt in his draper's shop in the Market Place. This was shortly after the fire of 1731. By 1790, six Blandford button merchants were listed in the Universal British directory – George Adams, Joseph James, Mrs Roe (widow), Tice & Fisher and Robert Fowle.

The governors of the Blandford Union Workhouse negotiated special terms with these merchants for buttons made by inmates; in 1764 John Jenkins produced 120 buttons in a day. Infirmity must have kept him in the workhouse, since his output would have earned him a good living outside. By 1770 three men and eleven women in the Workhouse were wholly employed in button making for the Case firm, and averaging ten gross per day between them.

The industry flourished until the middle of the 19th century, when Mr Ashton showed his patent button-making machine at the Great Exhibition of 1851. Within a decade the industry was virtually dead. Many of the button makers faced destitution and were forced to emigrate to the colonies. Some were absorbed as outworkers into the gloving industry, which was fairly extensive. Malachi Fisher was the last button merchant, and he died in 1874. His staff was instructed to burn remaining stocks, but some of them were preserved and have recently been exhibited in Blandford Museum.

The gloving industry increased in volume in the late 19th century and continued until well into the 20th century. The main buyers were the Yeovil glove factories, who lined and finished the product. Ensor & Southcombe of Milborne Port had a factory at Eagle House, Blandford, for many years and employed a large number of women there. This factory closed about December 1957.

Local tradesmen and merchants were fairly well organised in maintaining the trade of the town at least as early as 1755, when the Friendly Society of Tradesmen of Blandford, a sort of early Chamber of Trade, was functioning.

Ales, cider and wines have been made in Blandford throughout history. Ale was the basic drink for most people before tea and coffee came into common use, and its quality was strictly controlled by the manorial courts. As early as 1390 twelve men of Blandford appeared before the Court Leet of the manor charged with brewing ale and selling it contrary to regulations as to quality and measure.

Until the eighteenth century, innkeepers and estate owners generally, brewed their own ales and beers. In later years, the more successful of these began selling their products to other innkeepers and persons who were not customers at their inns, and it eventually became a full-time occupation for some. One of the earliest of these was William Clapcott, derscribed in 1796 as a 'beer and porter brewer'. In the same year Samuel Evans and Angell James were described as 'maltsters'. There were probably a good many earlier independent brewers in the town.

John Lewis Marsh, who had been landlord of the Kings Arms in Blandford, developed a successful brewing business in Bryanston Street in premises which are still standing (just!). He operated for about half a century and his business continued until 1938. By the 1860s another large brewery had grown up at Blandford St Mary. This was the business of John Hector (later Hector & Co). The Godwin family had a brewery at Durweston in mid-Victorian times. In 1848 Robert Fookes, a farmer, took over the Milton Abbas brewery of Charles Warne. Some of their bottles and jars can be seen at Christopher Fookes' Milton Abbas Museum at Park Farm. Another farmer, Charles Hall, founded a brewery at Ansty in 1777. His son, Robert, successfully developed the business and in 1847 took Mr G. E. I. Woodhouse into partnership. In 1882, as Hall & Woodhouse, they took over John Hector's Brewery, retaining their Ansty premises, as maltings, for making mineral waters and as storage. A large part of their Ansty premises are now used as the village hall. They acquired Godwins Brewery at Durweston in 1898, the Fontmell Magna Brewery in 1904, the Marnhull Brewery in 1912 and the Matthews Wyke Brewery at Gillingham in 1963, to become the largest employers of labour in the district except, of course, the Ministry of Defence at Blandford Camp.

A tour round the backs of the main streets of Blandford reveals many substantial barns and business premises of the past, and shows quite clearly that Blandford was a hive of industry in the 18th and 19th centuries, all being concealed from the view of the casual passer-by.

The first commercial bank to operate here was that founded in 1787 by John Dansey and William North Bastard, firstly in the Market Place and later at No 9 West Street. In 1843 the business was Bastard & Oak, William Coventry Oak having joined in partnership. He was joined by Charles Hastings Snow, and the old name retained until the business failed and payment was suspended in February 1858.

A branch of the Wilts & Dorset Bank was opened in West Street in February 1836 and later moved to part of the former Greyhound Inn. It later moved to premises in West Street formerly occupied by Dansey & Bastard's bank. It remained in business until taken over by Lloyds Bank Ltd in 1914, by which time it had again moved into the Market Place.

Pigot & Co's directory of 1830 shows Fryer, Andrews & Co in business in the Market Place, and in 1839 at No 5 West Street. This became a branch of the Wimborne, Poole & Blandford Bank, with partners William Fryer, Edwin Andrews, John Fryer and W. R. Fryer. It was taken over in 1841 by the National Provincial Bank, who moved to part of the old Greyhound Inn between 1845 and 1850. They took over and moved into former shop premises on the north side of the Market Place in 1979.

A one pound bank note of 1811 was recently found. It was issued at the Wimborne Bank and was payable at their offices at Poole or Blandford. This was a forerunner of the Wimborne, Poole and Blandford Bank.

James Bartlett, the last master of the old Free Grammar school, operated a savings bank from his home and the property eventually became known as Old Bank House. This was the Blandford Saving Bank established in 1818.

In the 19th century much local unemployment followed the merging of small farms, the effects of the Enclosure Acts and the introduction of agricultural machinery. In the first quarter of the century local landowners did their bit to relieve local distress by bringing in estate improvement schemes. Lord Portman employed over 100 Blandford and district men in the reclamation of Durweston common. The common was divided into seven fields, which were hand dug and sown and, although he spent over £10,000 on this project, his profit was negligible, but he had provided welcome employment over a long period and had permanently improved the land value.

From time to time agents from the colonies came to Blandford to recruit labour for Australia and Canada, and this greatly relieved the problem. The magistrates also adopted a policy of sending fit young men and women to serve sentences of transportation for quite minor offences. Many of these stayed in the colonies and became prosperous farmers and merchants.

The *Dorset County Chronicle* of May 1872 reported:

'For some time past, agricultural labourers, mostly young men, have flocked into Blandford from the neighbouring villages and arrangements have been made for obtaining situations for them at Manchester, Liverpool and other places. About 50 have gone off, and we hear more are on the eve of leaving. A gentleman from Texas (one of the Southern states of America) is expected shortly at Blandford, the purpose of whose visit is to engage 400 labourers to go to that country.'

Today it is not too clear why Blandford's livestock markets declined in the 1820s. The Borough Council ordered in 1821 that the pig market should be removed to the sheep market and in 1822 the cattle market was moved to Sheep Market Hill and the Tabernacle. Sales continued here for many years and later they were conducted at the Fair Field off Salisbury Road. Objections to street livestock came from residents living in these streets. There was a countrywide move for markets to be moved out of main streets, and in 1903 a saleyard for sheep horses and cattle was established by the Corporation in the Crown meadow, and the Thursday sales conducted by Senior, Godwin & Young were for many years well supported by farmers and merchants. No livestock markets are now held in the town.

The opening in recent times of an industrial estate at Blandford Heights has encouraged new business to the town, and has enabled many of Blandford's old established businesses to move out of the town centre and spread their wings. The most internationally well known of these is Alan Cobham Engineering Ltd, who manufacture products for all three United Kingdom fighting services, and many foreign services, British Gas, British Rail and, the National Coal Board. They are best known, perhaps, for their aircraft flight-refuelling products. Sir Alan J. Cobham, KBE, AFC, who was famous for his flying circus between the wars, was the pioneer of flight-refuelling, his first experiments having taken place in 1936. He died in 1973 and lies buried beside his wife in the churchyard at Tarrant Rushton.

Clock-face by John Spinney, c1760 (BM)

A NEW

CATALOGUE

OF THE

CIRCULATING LIBRARY,

OF

S. SIMMONDS,

BOOKSELLER, BOOKBINDER,

STATIONER & PRINTER,

AT THE HEAD OF THE MARKET-PLACE,

BLANDFORD, DORSET:

WHERE ARE SOLD

BOOKS IN ALL LANGUAGES;

STATIONARY WARES OF EVERY KIND;

Transparent and color'd Paper for Artificial Flowers;

A great Variety of plain and color'd PRINTS;

MUSICAL INSTRUMENTS & MUSIC OF ALL SORTS;

Strings, Reeds, Books of Instructions, &c. for ditto.

Most of the Genuine Patent Medicines that are Advertised in the News-papers, &c.

Oil'd Lawn, Ditto and Plain Silk UMBRELLAS;

PERFUMERY from the First Shops in LONDON.

POMATUM at 6d. and 1s. per Roll or Pot.

A great Variety of Ivory, Bone, Horn and Tortoiseshell Combs, and Fishing Tackle, from the best Makers in this Kingdom.

SPECTACLES, Temple, Common and Double Joint.

Convex and Concave READING-GLASSES.

STAMPT PAPER, PARCHMENT, &c.

AS CHEAP AS IN LONDON.

SIMMONDS, TYP.

Early Blandford library notice c1800. (BM)

BLANDFORD.

NOVEMBER

Sheep Fair.

NOTICE is hereby given to all whom it may concern, that the above Fair which has beeen heretofore kept in the Town of Blandford, will (with the consent of the Bailiff and Burgesses) this year be held on Friday, the 8th Day of November next, in a field near the Town, in the possession of Mr. S. Smith, adjoining Salisbury Street.

Application for Pens, to be made as usual to W. Kendall, which must be paid for when taken.

Dated, 28th October, 1822

OPPOSITE LEFT: Blandford buttons; (BM) RIGHT: halfpenny token of W. Sanger, Blandford 1798; (BM) BELOW: notice re Sheep Fair, 1822. (DCM) ABOVE: Sheepmarket Hill, 1977 with reconstructed cattle market, (BM) and BELOW: Market Place about 1895. (BM)

WADE BROS

HALL & WOODHOUSE L^{TD} THE BREWERY
HALL & WOODHOUSE L^{TD}
THE BREWERY BLANDFORD
SPEED 5M.P.H

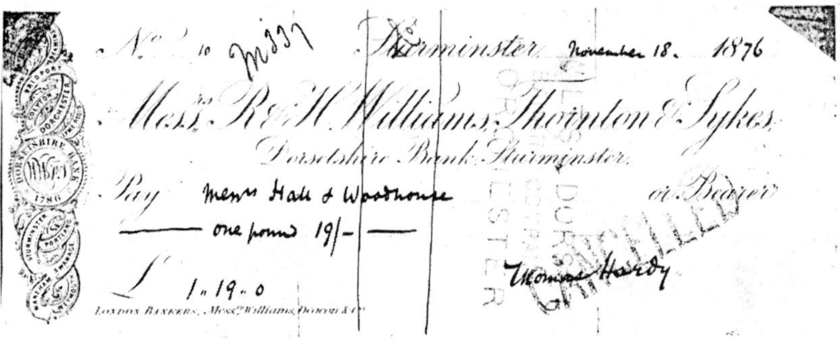

No. 10 M337 Sturminster November 18. 1876

Messrs R. & H. Williams, Thornton & Sykes,

Dorsetshire Bank Sturminster.

Pay Messrs Hall & Woodhouse or Bearer

one pound 19/-

£ 1.19.0

London Bankers, Messrs Williams, Deacon & Co

Thomas Hardy

CANCELLED

OPPOSITE ABOVE: Market Place about 1912; (JG) CENTRE: staff at Hall & Woodhouse bottle beer store, c1912; (DW) BELOW: one of their steam lorries at Blandford St Mary. (HW) ABOVE: Ansty Brewery (now village hall), (HW) and BELOW: Thomas Hardy's cheque 1876. (HW)

LEFT: Local wine merchants' jar (early 19th c). (WG) RIGHT: 18 Market Place 1910; (DW) BELOW: J. L. Marsh's Brewery, Bryanston Street. (BM)

ABOVE: The George family, grocers in Blandford for several generations; (BM) BELOW: E. D. Horsey, Salisbury Street 1906. (DW)

· Moderate Use of Stimulants !

Physical Improvement ! !

Eminent Doctors' Opinions :

Sir James Paget, Bart., F.R.C.S.,D.C.L.,LL.D.,F.R.S.

"As for the opinion of the Medical Profession, they are, by a vast majority in favour of a moderate habitual use of alcoholic drinks, and there are sufficient reasons for believing that such an habitual use is on the whole generally beneficial."

Sir William Gull, Bart., M.D., F.R.C.P.,D.C.L.,F.R.S.

"For men working hard, beer is a good form of food, to be recommended as a light feeding material."

T Lauder Brunton, M.D., F.R.C.P., F.R.S.

"Alcohol is a true food."

Albert J. Bernays, Ph.D.

"A glass of Beer, when the day's work is done, can do no possible harm

R. Brudenell Carter, F.R.C.S.

"I do not hesitate to say that the advocates of total abstinence are mistaken. I affirm, alike from my own experience and from that of others, that there are some to whom it is a necessity if they are to exert the full measure of their power,"

Alfred B. Garrod, M.D., F.R.C.P., F.R.S.

"The majority of adults can take a moderate quantity of alcohol not only with impunity, but often with advantage."

Sir Dyce Duckworth, M.D., LL.D., F.R.C.P.

Hon. Ph. to H.R.H the Prince of Wales, now His Majesty the King

"I believe the use of alcohol to be beneficial to humanity. In strict moderation I see nothing harmful, but on the contrary much that is beneficial in the present stage of our civilisation."

The late Rt. Hon. W. E. Gladstone said:

"Bitter Beer was a divine drink."

Tea taken in excess has been proved to be more harmful than Malt and Hop Beers in moderation.

Many very aged Persons in this Town and Neighbourhood are living instances of the beneficial effects of Moderate use of Stimulants.

Drink

MARSH'S Pure Malt and Hop ALES

And Live for ever.

The Brewery, Blandford.

J. L. Marsh advertising matter, 1907. (BM)

ABOVE: Southern end of Whitecliff Mill Street, (BM) and BELOW: International Stores when in Salisbury Street, 1920s. (BM)

Some of Blandford's 17th century tradesmen's tokens. (BM)

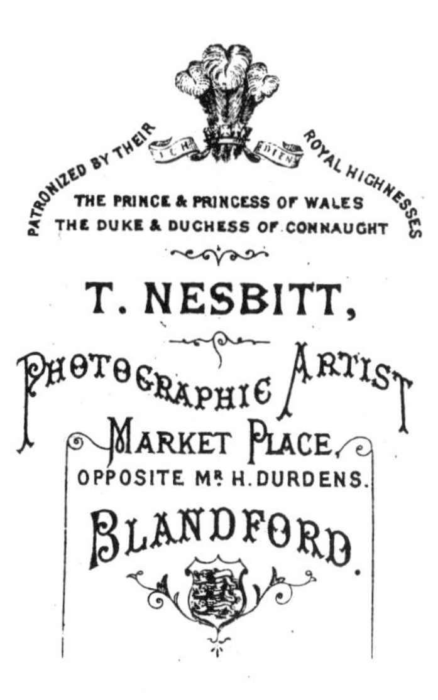

LEFT: Thomas Nesbitt probably took a lot of the photographs appearing in this book; (BM) RIGHT: Blandford Shopping Week programme 1928; (BM) BELOW: Walt. Bridle 1906. (DW)

ABOVE: Electrocuted sheep at Thornicomb 1914, and BELOW: Mr Hurley's Trojan van, c1930. (BM)

O.H.M.S.

Blandford has enjoyed a long and interesting association with the military, who for generations have favoured the downlands north-east of the town as sites for at first temporary, and later permanent, military establishments. In 1757 Major General James Wolfe reviewed his troops there and their training included frequent mock battles involving ascents of the Hod and Hambledon hills. A participant made the following comment:

'We had a general review of our forces yesterday on Blandford Down to the great entertainment of the ignorant spectators, though according to my judgement we do not deserve even their approbation. There are officers who had the vanity and presumption to applaud our operations, bad as they were, but I hope the General saw our defects and will supply a remedy, without which I think we are in imminent danger of being cut to pieces in our first engagement.'

Although 'the General' lost his own life at the battle of Quebec in 1759, his troops were victorious, thus ensuring the conquest of Canada.

On 17 June 1771 the *Salisbury & Winchester Journal* reported a review of the Dorsetshire Regiment of Militia by Colonel George Pitt and added:

'After the review a grand entertainment was given by the Colonel, to the corps, and upwards of a hundred gentlemen, at the new assembly room and the whole concluded with a ball given to the ladies, which was very numerous and splendid.'

In 1804 a defence survey was made throughout the country. The Blandford Division had nine deputy lieutenants, 29 tithings, 1,586 men between the ages of 15 and 60 capable of service, 43,058 oxen, cows, sheep etc, 250 riding horses, 315 draught horses and 474 waggons and carts, and long estimates of food likely to be available.

The Dorset Imperial Yeomanry was founded in 1794 with a troop at Blandford and functioned throughout the Napoleonic wars. It was revived in 1830 because of fears of a general uprising of the peasantry.

In 1815 the Duke of Wellington inspected his troops at Blandford, prior to setting off for the campaign which was to lead to the battle of Waterloo and the end of the war with France.

The Dorset Rifle Volunteer Corps was established in 1859 with a company at Blandford. They were originally formed for coastal defence duties but later distinguished themselves in action in South Africa in 1902.

During the Boer war a large military training establishment was set up on the site of the present Blandford camp and, between then and 1914, it was used by yeomanry and other territorial units as a training camp for instruction in general duties, saddlery, farriery, marksmanship and other ancillary skills.

A memorial in Blandford Forum parish church tells us that George Vince, AB RN, born at Blandford on 20 September 1880, was on the exploration ship *Discovery* which went to the Antarctic under Captain Robert Scott. Mr Vince died as a result of a fall over an icecliff into the sea at Ross, Ireland on 11 March 1902.

The 1914-1918 war saw the erection of the first hutted camp for the accommodation of the Collingwood and Anson battalions of the Royal Naval Division – at its peak there were something like 30,000 men and civilians there. Rupert Brooke, the poet, served there and carried out menial duties but found time to write his sonnet *The Soldier,* including the famous lines:

'If I should die, think only this of me
That there's some corner of a foreign field
That is for ever England. There shall be
In that rich earth a richer dust concealed . . .'

One of his letters tells how he spent a Christmas at Blandford Camp looking after drunken stokers, and he sent a telegram asking a friend to send mincepies and cakes for 60 men immediately because the food was so terrible. He unfortunately perished with the majority of those of the division who served at Gallipoli in 1915. Prior to the departure of the battalions from Blandford they were reviewed by George V and Winston Churchill, then First Lord of the Admiralty.

Blandford was delighted when, in 1918, it was announced that one of its sons, Jack Thomas Counter, had been awarded the Victoria Cross. He was created an Honorary Freeman of the Borough on 19 June 1918.

The second world war brought thousands of troops, evacuated from Dunkirk and elsewhere, to Blandford Camp, to await reposting. The camp was later occupied by American forces, who converted part of it into a military hospital. The 1st United States Infantry Division had their headquarters at Langton House, since demolished, and Captain Quentin Roosevelt, a nephew of the United States President, was married at Blandford church in 1944. Roosevelt Park at the camp was named after his family. He was there from 8 November 1943 until the unit sailed from Portland Roads on 5 April 1944 for Omaha beach. While at Blandford Camp, the unit was visited by General Eisenhower, Field Marshall Montgomery and comedian Bob Hope.

Further east, the Tarrant Rushton airfield was constructed, and it was thence that planes and soldiers were despatched for the Normandy landings and later, to face action at Arnhem.

For fifteen years or so after this war the camp was used by a variety of territorial and regular units. In 1960 the Royal Corps of Signals began their move to the camp followed by the School of Signals in 1967. Blandford town has always benefitted from the business and employment generated over the years by the camp. The Freedom of Entry to the Town and Borough was bestowed upon the Royal Corps of Signals in 1972. A similar honour had previously been bestowed upon the Dorset Regiment in 1955. This was extended at a ceremony in 1983 to include the Devon & Dorset Regiment.

Blandford did not suffer as greatly as many places during the two world wars, but the town's sons and daughters were not slow to answer the call to service of their country, and the town's war memorials record the names of the many that did not return.

Blandford men in West Street about to leave for the war, August 1914. (BM)

For the County of *Dorset*

Dorset } WE *The Revd Wm Chafin* and *The Revd Geo: Fito Brice Clerke* ~~Esquires~~, two of the Justices of the Peace in and for this County, do hereby certify, that *Geo: Chapman* hath voluntarily entered himself in the Service of His Majesty's *Navy* for the Parish of *Blandford &c* — and that his Discription is as under-written:

Number of the Certificate.	Name.	Place of Birth or lawful Settlement.	Age.	Calling.
No. 1	*George Chapman*	*Blandford Dorset*	*18*	*Labourer*

And we do further certify, that the Sum of *Fifteen* — Pounds, hath been agreed to be paid as a Bounty to the said *Geo: Chapman* on his entering into such Service; And we do hereby direct, that the Sum of *Five* — Pounds, Part thereof, shall be paid to the said — *Geo: Chapman* — at his Request, at the time of his Enrolment; And we do further certify, that we have ordered the Overseers of the said Parish of *Blandford* — to pay into the Hands of *John* [illegible] the Treasurer of the said County of *Dorset* within the Space of Fourteen Days from the Date hereof, the Sum of *Ten* Pounds, being the Residue of the said Bounty, to be applied as the Act in such Case directs. Given under our Hands and Seals, this *fifteen* — Day of *December* in the Year of our Lord *1796* —

Wm Chafin

Geo: Fito Brice

ABOVE: Bounty certificate 1796; (DRO) LEFT: officer of the Dorset Rifle Volunteers c1855, (BM) and RIGHT: Jack T. Counter, VC. (BM)

ABOVE: Troops at Blandford Camp, c1916; (BM) BELOW: George V and Churchill arrive at Blandford Station *en route* to Blandford Camp, 1915. (BM)

ABOVE: Wareham & Arscott's van at Blandford Camp, c1911; (DW) CENTRE: Blandford & District men in India 1915, (BM) and BELOW: Queen's Own Dorset Yeomanry camp at Blandford c1910. (BM)

ABOVE: Disaster in Whitecliffe Mill Street in 1951, (DF) CENTRE: members of the Royal Naval Division at Blandford Camp 1914, and BELOW: Jersey postage stamp issued 1971 to commemorate 50th anniversary of the British Legion. (BM)

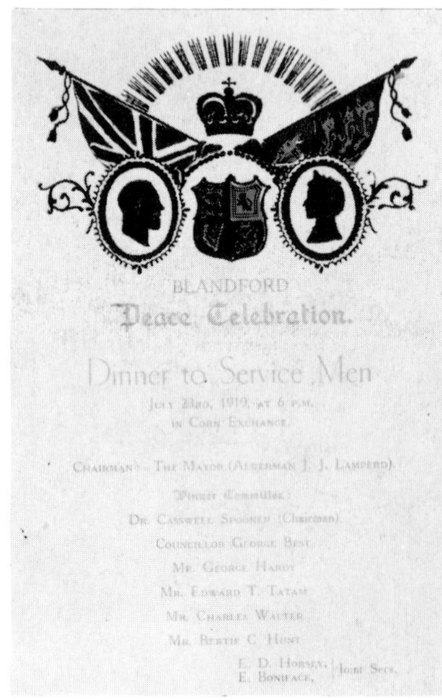

BLANDFORD
Peace Celebration.

Dinner to Service Men
July 23rd, 1919, at 6 p.m.
in Corn Exchange.

Chairman – The Mayor (Alderman J. J. Lamperd).

Dinner Committee:
Dr. Caswell Spooner (Chairman)
Councillor George Best
Mr. George Hardy
Mr. Edward T. Tatam
Mr. Charles Walter
Mr. Bertie C. Hunt
E. D. Horsey, } Joint Secs.
E. Boniface,

ABOVE: Despatch rider, Blandford Camp, 1916; (DW) LEFT: Blandford Peace celebrations, dinner for service men, 1919; (BM) RIGHT: Armistice celebrations 1914-18 war: Mrs Emily Knight and Mr Frank Knight, proprietor, 3 Choughs, West Street, with policemen and painter.

ABOVE: Comrades of the Great War. Langton House 1920; (SJ) CENTRE: Blandford Home Guard c1943, (DW) BELOW: RAF airfield, Tarrant Rushton, 1945. (BM)

ABOVE: Freedom of Borough of Blandford Forum granted to the Dorset Regiment 1955, (BM) and BELOW: Blandford Ambulance Corps, 1912/13. (DW)

Patterns of Change

From the Middle Ages to the 1731 fire the pattern of life had not much changed. The ordinary people of the town and local traders, merchants, farmers and well-to-do residents, had few occasions on which they needed to travel more than 30 miles or so from home and, when they did, their journeys were fraught with dangers and not occasions to which to look forward. The roads in all directions had been neglected since Roman times but, as those around Blandford were over chalk downlands, they were rarely impassable, and this contributed to the town's popularity as a place of business and of residence, being roughly equidistant with Poole, Dorchester and Salisbury.

Under an Act of 1535, the responsibility for repairing roads became the duty of the parish, which annually appointed an officer to take charge of the work. He was usually called the hayward or surveyor and was obliged to accept the office, find a substitute, or suffer a penalty. He had to organise the necessary labour to keep the parish roads in good order and had the power to set all able-bodied men to work for usually four, but sometimes up to eight days a year.

In 1691 a further Act was passed transferring the responsibility from the parish to the magistrates, who were empowered to levy a rate to pay for road repairs; this resulted in some improvement. It was not until the last decade of the 17th century that Parliament granted powers to collect tolls on certain roads to pay for their maintenance. The first of these 'turnpikes', as they became known, were intended only as a temporary measure to bring them up to reasonable standards. Turnpike acts were obtained from Parliament in favour of trustees, usually the local landowners, authorising them to levy the tolls. These were payable at toll-gates erected at entrances to towns or at important junctions, local examples being at Tarrant Hinton and Blandford St Mary. The principal trusts concerning Blandford were the Harnham, Blandford & Dorchester Trust from 1753, covering the greater part of the A35 Salisbury to Dorchester road, and the Blandford and Poole Trust, from 1764, which undertook the turnpiking of the road via Charlton Marshall, Sturminster Marshall and Corfe Mullen to Poole. This turnpike was eventually discontinued in favour of the road via Shapwick and Badbury Rings operated by the Blandford & Wimborne Trust, which continued until 1882. The only real objectors were the local farmers who, as the main users, objected to tolls. These road improvements had the effect of putting Blandford on the map as an important coaching town on the main London to Exeter road. The coming of the mail and stage coaches resulted in considerable extensions at the Crown and the Greyhound, Blandford's principal coaching inns; much of the extensive stabling and outbuildings can still be seen at the rear of these premises. The comings and going of coaches were frequent and work was provided for many. Coaches ran daily to London and the West Country and several coaches a week ran to Southampton and Portsmouth.

Coaches unfortunately attracted highwaymen, and there are numerous records of their activities in the Blandford area. In 1691 Jack Withrington and Thomas Cox, both Blandford born, were hanged at Tyburn after conviction for highway robbery. Withrington asserted that his four elder brothers had all died on the scaffold. It was still going on in the early 19th century, for a sermon was preached at Blandford on 13 August 1820 by Rev C. J. Hoare on the two Blandford brothers, John and Moses Blanchard, who had been executed for highway robbery after trial at Dorchester Assizes.

In the 1790s a scheme was mooted which, if brought to fruition, might have altered the status of Blandford for better or worse. This was the proposed Dorset and Somerset canal, which went onto the drawing board at the height of the canal era. Various routes were discussed, including one from Bath through Frome, Wincanton, Henstridge, Stalbridge, Sturminster Newton, King's Stag, Mappowder, Ansty, Puddletown, Wareham and down to Poole. Another plan under discussion varied the route to run via Sturminster Newton, Shillingstone and Blandford. This was finally selected by the trustees of the scheme, and interested landowners, after numerous meetings at the Crown in Blandford. Objections were subsequently raised and it was ultimately decided that the route from Bath would terminate at Shillingstone near Blandford, with the final stage via Blandford to Poole abandoned. An Act of Parliament of 24 March 1796 gave authority. There followed further lengthy delays in construction. A start was made at the Somerset end, but technical and geological problems intervened, and further difficulties experienced with landowners. Finance was also a problem, for investors began to get cold feet. It became apparent that railway mania was imminent, with possibilities of a better service and improved dividends. Had the scheme started 25 years earlier it might have been completed as far as Blandford, but whether this would have been much of a stimulus to trade is now difficult to assess. The scheme was finally abandoned and the shares became practically worthless.

The coming of the railways also sounded the death knell of the coaching trade. As the trains came nearer, the coaching industry diminished, the local coach owners finally restricted to taking Blandford people to the nearest rail connections. Another blow was The almost overnight cessation of the need for hotel accommodation.

The first railway to reach Blandford was the Dorset Central, which was a narrow gauge track of 10¾ miles from Wimborne on the South Western line. It was authorised by an Act of Parliament of 29 July 1856. On 13 November 1856 Lady Smith of the Down House, Blandford St Mary, cut the first turf from the field over which the track would be laid. The line was completed and opened on 1 October 1860 but the terminus was then over the river at Blandford St Mary. A public luncheon was held at Blandford Corn Exchange to mark the occasion.

In 1862 the Somerset Central Railway and the Dorset Central Railway joined forces to become the Somerset & Dorset Railway and, on the line reaching Blandford Forum, a railway station was constructed there and opened in 1863. This was a great blessing as it absorbed a good many unemployed, and extended local horizons. It certainly facilitated trade and travel but surprisingly did not bring about any increase in population, or any substantial increases in the numbers of businesses, business premises, private housing or any general development. The population, which was 3,850 in 1901, was actually less than when the census of 1861 was made, showing the population at 3,900. No doubt the railway speeded up the general depopulation of the countryside and of small towns in favour of industrial centres. Numerous smaller stations and halts were erected in villages in the area which enabled people to come in by train to shop and children to attend Blandford schools.

A small branch line was constructed in the latter part of the 1914-18 war. This branched off the main Somerset & Dorset line south of Blandford's East Street arches. It crossed the Badbury Rings road about 350 yards up from St Leonard's Chapel and ran parallel to and north of that road, before curving across Hungry Down and Snows Down, passing through Bingleton Wood and on to Blandford Camp where, at that time, some 20,000 to 30,00 troops were stationed. It remained in use for only a few years, when the track was taken up and the bed used as a dump for Blandford's domestic rubbish. The new Blandford by-pass, in course of construction as I write, cuts across the line of the old track to reveal much of this old rubbish, to the delight of local bottle and treasure hunters, who have been given temporary access.

The village carriers continued to bring in goods for sale in the market, to buy goods for those in their villages not able to travel and to carry passengers with business to transact in Blandford.

The coming of the motor car had no serious effect on the railway service until after the second world war. Its coming was not welcomed in Blandford. Mr G. W. Holdway, late of Child Okeford, who was at school at Blandford, recorded this account of one of the first motor cars to be seen in the town – this was in 1895:

'The same year at Blandford I saw the first motor car. It belonged to a circus family visiting the town and created a great deal of excitement. It had solid rubber tyres about half an inch in diameter. It was driven through the streets at about four miles per hour. A man briskly waving a red flag trotted about 100 yards ahead (which was compulsory by law at this time). About 100 cheering children ran behind. The car made a noise like a threshing machine. The horses both old and young bolted up side streets and would not face this new invention which has since displaced them.'

By the 1960s less and less use was made of the railway for both passengers and goods and the Somerset & Dorset line closed on 7 March 1966 to passenger traffic and on 12 February 1967 to goods. It was affectionately known as the 'Swift and Delightful' by those who operated it and the 'Slow and Dirty' by those who travelled on it. The site of the station and yards is now taken up for housing, but a few relics of its 100 years of service have thoughtfully been incorporated into the landscaping. Long stretches of the track are also retained as amenity land. The closure inevitably led to further congestion of the town's roads, particularly during the summer months, but it is hoped that the new by-pass will effectively overcome the problem, with damage to the town's buildings substantially reduced.

The 19th century saw a number of new buildings and services to improve the quality of life, and death, including the lighting of the town by gas in 1837, the provision of a new cemetery in Salisbury Road in 1855, the building of the present Corn Exchange in 1858, where farmers and merchants conducted their business, and the erection of a new Union Workhouse in Salisbury Road in 1859 with a new police station opposite.

Electric lighting was available in the town before the 1914/18 war from the Dorset Electric Supply Co Ltd, and in the 1920s by the Blandford Forum & District Electric Supply Co Ltd. Prior to nationalisation, the town was supplied by the Bournemouth & Poole Electricity Supply Co Ltd.

As to newspapers Blandford had difficulty in maintaining its own publication. The longest run was that of the *Blandford Express*, published from Whitecliff Mill Street, from 1869 to 1894. This was followed by the *Blandford Gazette and Three Shires Advertiser* which appeared only from August to December 1903. The *Express* had some competition between 1885 and 1892 from *the Blandford Weekly*

News and between 1874 and 1886 from the *Blandford, Wimborne & Poole Telegram.* Early in this century the town was served by the *Blandford & East Dorset Herald* and throughout these perids the town and district were served by the *Western Gazette* and, in the earlier period, by the *Salisbury & Winchester Journal.*

British Telecom cannot say when the public telephone first came to Blandford, neither have they a directory of the first subscribers. This is because, from the late 1880s, the service operated under the monopoly of the National Telephone Company which had swallowed up a number of smaller companies. They were taken over by the Post Office in 1911. It seems that the Blandford subscribers retained their National numbers when the first post office exchange was opened at the West Street post office.

Early in 1883 a cottage hospital was built, at the expense of the Hon Miss Portman, adjoining the Corner Coffee House near the junction of Whitecliff Mill Street with Salisbury Street. There is a record that a man injured in a waggon accident at Tarrant Hinton in March 1883 was brought to that address. During the period 1885-1887 the building was known as the Nurse House; it was not, apparently, then accepting in-patients, who were sent to Bath, Weymouth, Bournemouth or Dorchester. In April 1888 plans were mde for the Nurse House to revert to its original use as a cottage hospital, but it is doubtful whether in fact it ever did more than treat casualties. In December of that year a new cottage hospital was opened at Picket Close, the original foundation being by the Viscountess Portman and the Hon L. E. Portman. The Portman family for many years provided the matron and the nurses. This was their stated intention:

'This hospital is principally intended for the necessitous poor of Blandford and those parishes in the neighbourhood which have no institution of the kind within easy reach of them — such patients are admitted free of charge.'

This was but one of the many charitable foundations and benefits provided by the Portman family for the people of Blandford and district, many of whom were their workpeople and tenants. Their mansion at Bryanston had been sold in 1927 for use as a public school, and in July 1950 Viscount Portman handed over his Dorset estate of 3,800 acres to the Commissioners of Inland Revenue as part-payment of duty levied after the death of his father, the seventh Viscount, in 1948.

A great deal of illness in the town had, for generations, been due to inadequate sanitary facilities and unsafe water. This, following numerous outbreaks of cholera and smallpox, was repeatedly highlighted by local medical men, who stressed the dangers of 'the of piped water in 1894 by the Blandford Waterworks Company. Even then it was a long time before many cottages were connected to the supply and, even after the 1939/45 war, there were many without flush toilets. Quite a lot of elderly people were obstinate about it and expressed themselves as horrified at the idea of having a lavatory inside the house! The public sewers were here in the 1920s.

These various improvements made Blandford a happier place in which to live and it had become quite up-to-date, compared with other small towns, for its time. It still retains its old country-town serenity with plenty of old-established private businesses using their original shop fronts of Victorian vintage, shopkeepers who still have time to talk to their customers and a generally unhurried approach to most things — long may it so remain. The visits in 1982 of the Princess Anne and the Prime Minister, Mrs Margaret Thatcher, did much to help put Blandford on the map, and it is hoped that those interested in tourism will succeed in bringing many more visitors to Blandford in the future.

GOULD'S

LONDON AND BLANDFORD

FLY WAGONS,

Leave Gerrard's Hall, Basing Lane, Cheapside; Spread Eagle, Piccadilly, every Tuesday, Thursday, and Saturday Evenings, for Salisbury, Blandford, Dorchester, Weymouth, Wareham, and all parts of the West of England.

Leave his Office, East-street, Blandford, (late Russells and Co's,) every Tuesday, Thursday, and Saturday Evenings, for London, calling at Smith aud Dawes' Office, Brown Street, Salisbury.

W. GOULD begs to return his best thanks to the Public, for past favors, and hopes, by regularity and dispatch of business, to meet a continuance of that patronage he has so long been favored with.

Printed by F. CLEMENCE, Bookseller, &c., BLANDFORD.

Early road transport notice c1860.(BM)

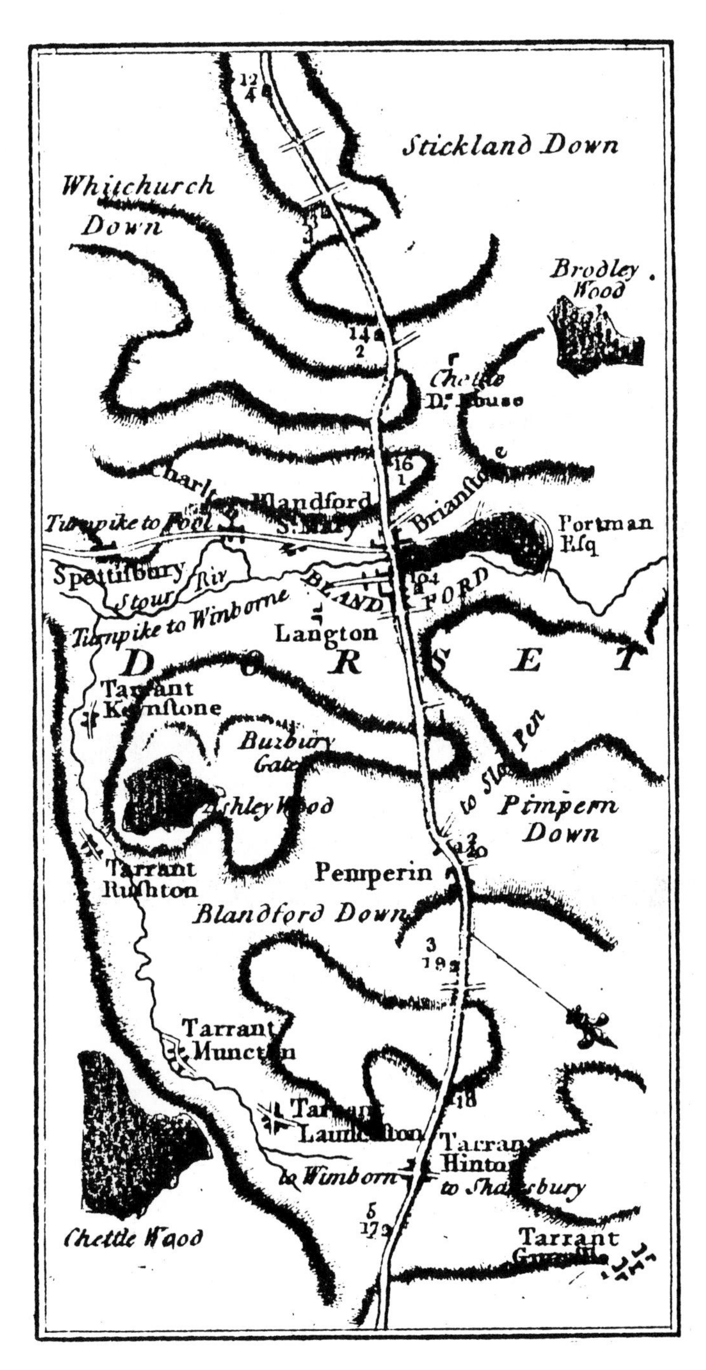

Extract from Carey's survey of the London to Exeter Road, 1782. (BM)

ANNO TRICESIMO SEXTO

Georgii III. Regis.

C A P. XLVII.

An Act for making a Navigable Canal from or near *Gain's Crofs*, in the Parifh of *Shillingfton Okeford*, in the County of *Dorfet*, to communicate with the *Kennet* and *Avon* Canal, at or near *Widbrook*, in the County of *Wilts*, and alfo a certain Navigable Branch from the intended Canal.

[24th *March* 1796.]

Preamble.

WHEREAS the making and maintaining a Navigable Canal for Boats, Barges, and other Veffels, from or near a Place called *Gain's Crofs*, within the Parifh of *Shillingfton Okeford*, in the County of *Dorfet*, to join and communicate with the *Kennet* and *Avon* Canal, at or near *Widbrook*, in the Parifh of *Bradford*, in the County of *Wilts*; and alfo the Navigable Branch herein-after defcribed, from the faid intended Canal, will open an eafy and convenient Communication with many confiderable manufacturing Towns and Places in the Country through which the fame are intended to pafs, and alfo with the extenfive Collieries near *Mendip*, in the County of *Somerfet*; and will render the Conveyance of Goods, Wares, and Merchandize, Coal, Stone, Slate, Flags, Lime, Limeftone, Timber, and other Things, lefs expenfive than at prefent, and will be of great publick Utility: But the fame

6 Z 2 cannot

Preamble to Dorset and Somerset Canal Act 1796. (BM)

Spooner, 

Blandford.

ROYAL MAIL

AND

GENERAL COACH OFFICE

FOR LIGHT SAFETY COACHES.

The REGULATOR LIGHT COACH, for LONDON, every Morning at a quarter before 1 o'Clock, to the Swan with Two Necks, Lad Lane; calls at Dyson's Black Bear, Picadilly.

The MAGNET COACH, for LONDON, every Morning, at a quarter before 8 o'Clock, to the Swan two Necks, Lad Lane, and Saracen's Head, Snow Hill, calls at Hatchet's Hotel, and Dyson's Black Bear, Picadilly.

The ROYAL MAIL, every Evening at 5 o'Clock for London.

The PORTSMOUTH & BRIGHTON COACH, for Southampton, every Monday, Wednesday, and Friday Afternoons, at half-past three.

The ROYAL PILOT, for Bath and Bristol, every Tuesday, Thursday, and Saturday Mornings, at a quarter before 8 o'Clock. From Bath are Coaches to Gloucester, Hereford, Worcester, Cheltenham, Birmingham, Shrewsbury, and Holyhead.

The REGULATOR, for Exeter and Plymouth, every Morning, at half-past 5 o'Clock; *(through to Plymouth the same Evening.*

The ROYAL MAIL, for Exeter and Falmouth, every Morning at 9 o'Clock; *arrives at Bridport in time for the Mail thro' Beaminster, Crewkerne, and Taunton.*

The SOUTHAMPTON COACH, every Tuesday, Thursday, and Saturday Mornings, at 11 o'Clock, for Exeter, Barnstaple, Teignmouth, Sidmouth, and Devonport.

A COACH to Weymouth, every Morning, at 5 o'Clock, and every Evening at 6 o'Clock.

A LIGHT COACH to Poole, every Monday, Wednesday, and Friday Evenings, at 6 o'Clock.

N. B. The Proprietors of the above Coaches will not be accountable for any article whatever, if lost or damaged, exceeding the value of £5, unless entered as such, and paid for accordingly.

*** *The greatest care will be taken, the lowest rate charged, and the utmost expedition used in the delivery of all parcels booked at the above office. Orders by letter duly attended to.*

OAKLEY, PRINTER, BLANDFORD.

ROUTES FROM BLANDFORD.

TO LONDON THROUGH STOCKBRIDGE.

			MILES.
Woodyats	*Shaftesbury Arms*	BROOKS	12
Salisbury	*White Hart*	JONES	10
Stockbridge	*Hotel*	KING	15
Popham Lane	*Wheat Sheaf*	ROBLIN	15
Murrel Green	*Wellesly Arms*	WEBB	14
Bagshot	*White Hart*	MARLIN	12
Egham	*King's Head*	DORE	9
Hounslow	*George*	CHARLTON	9
London			10
		MILES	106

TO LONDON THROUGH ANDOVER

FROM SALISBURY.

To Andover	*White Hart*	MILES	18
Worting	*White Hart*	READ	16
Murrel Green	*Wellesly Arms*	WEBB	18
Bagshot	*White Hart*	MARLIN	12
Egham	*King's Head*	DORE	9
Hounslow	*George*	CHARLTON	9
London			10
		MILES	84

TO EXETER AND DEVONPORT.

Dorchester	*King's Arms*	OLIVER	16
Bridport	*Bull*	TUCKER	15
Axminster	*George*	STEVENS	12
Honiton	*Golden Lion*	WEBBER	9
Exeter	*New London Inn*	CLENCH	16
Chudleigh	*Clifford Arms*	WESTON	10
Ashburton	*Golden Lion*	JEFFERY	10
Ivybridge	*Rogers Arms*	WINSOR	13
Devonport	*King's Arms*	ELLIOTT	13
		MILES	114

TO SOUTHAMPTON.

Wimborne	*New Inn*	PURKIS	10
Ringwood	*White Hart*	TRAVERS	10
Stoney-Cross	*Compton Arms*	TRAVERS	9
Southampton	*Dolphin & George*		11
		MILES	40

Coaching notice issued by Crown Hotel Blandford, c1825.

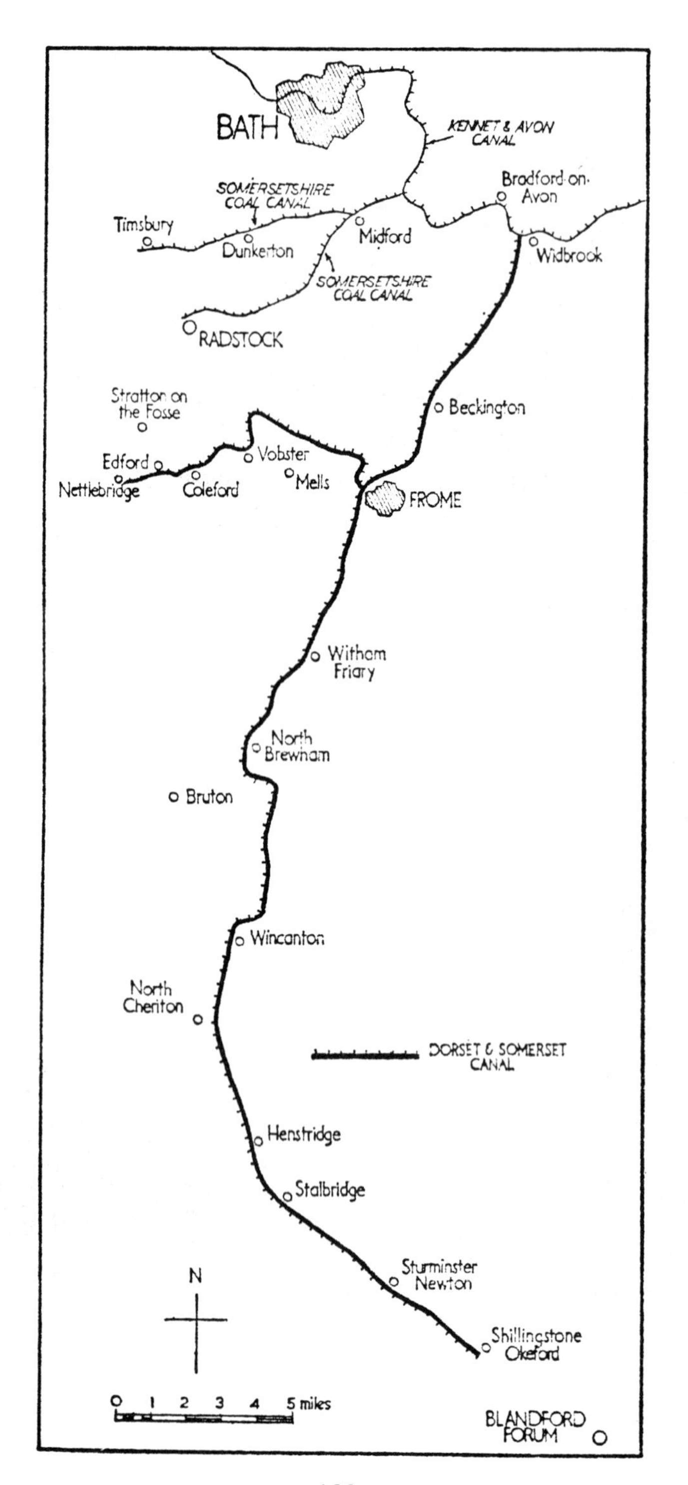
BATH
KENNET & AVON CANAL
SOMERSETSHIRE COAL CANAL
Bradford-on-Avon
Timsbury
Dunkerton
Midford
Widbrook
SOMERSETSHIRE COAL CANAL
RADSTOCK
Stratton on the Fosse
Beckington
Edford
Vobster
Nettlebridge
Coleford
Mells
FROME
Witham Friary
North Brewham
Bruton
Wincanton
North Cheriton
DORSET & SOMERSET CANAL
Henstridge
Stalbridge
Sturminster Newton
N
Shillingstone Okeford
0 1 2 3 4 5 miles
BLANDFORD FORUM

NOTICE.

BLANDFORD
GAS AND COKE
COMPANY.

Persons feeling interested in the establishment of Gas Works in this Town, are respectfully informed that a Meeting is intended to be held tomorrow Morning, at the Town-Hall, at eleven o'Clock, for the purpose of submitting a certain portion of shares in the undertaking to the Public, and for making final arrangements for erecting the Works immediately.

W. M. Stears, Contractor,

***Blandford*, 9th. *Month*, 14th. 1836.**

SHIPP, PRINTER, BLANDFORD.

ABOVE: Notice re establishment of gas works 1836, (DCM) and BELOW: town approach before the motor car, about 1890; (JG) OPPOSITE: projected route of Dorset & Somerset Canal. (BM)

ABOVE: Interior of old Post Office in West Street 1934, (BM) and CENTRE: staff at new Post Office at The Tabernacle 1935; (BM) BELOW: *West Country* class engine No 34107, Blandford Forum. (BM)

ABOVE: Blandford Forum station c1930; (BM) CENTRE: and in 1967; (BM) BELOW: last photograph of the East Street railway bridges. (SJ)

LEFT: Tom Cousins, 40 years a postman at Blandford; (BM) RIGHT: a nostalgic scene from the 30's — Whitecliff Mill Hill, Blandford, and BELOW: Blandford Museum, 1983. (SJ).

Bibliography

V. J. Adams *A Thousand Years of Blandford History* 1983
T. F. Almack *A Village Heritage (Blandford St. Mary)* 1961
A. R. Bayley *The Great Civil War in Dorset 1642-1660* 1910
J. Bugler & J. Drew*Roman Dorset, D.N.A.S.* 1974
J. W. Brailsford *Hod Hill* vol i. 1962 vol ii. 1968
J. H. Betty *Dorset* 1974
J. H. Betty *The Landscape of Wessex* 1980
H. N. Colvin *The Bastards of Blandford* 1948
K. R. Clew *The Dorset & Somerset Canal* 1971
B. G. Cox *The Hospital & Chapel of St. Leonard, Blandford Forum* 1983
B. G. Box *The 17th Century Token Coinage of Blandford Forum* 1983
H. S. L. Dewar (ed.) *The Thomas Rackett Papers – Dorset Record Society* 1965
J. E. Dalton (ed.) *The Manuscripts of St. George's Chapel, Windsor* 1957
R. Douch *Handbook of Local History – Dorset* 1962
Dorset Natural History & Archaeological Society – proceedings.
N. H. Field & J. Bugler *The Ancient Monuments of Dorset – a definitive list* 1972
J. K. Galpine (ed.), J. H. Hasserey (ed.) *The Georgian Garden, an 18th Century Nurseryman's catalogue* 1983
L. M. Grouble & M. C. B. Bowden DNAS *The Archaeology of Rural Dorset, Past Present and Future* 1982
L. V. Grinsell *The Archaeology of Wessex* 1958
L. V. Grinsell *Dorset Barrows* 1959 DNAS and supplement 1982
R. Good *The Old Roads of Dorset* 1966
D. Hawkins *Cranborne Chase* 1980
C. F. C. Hawkes, Arch.Jol.civ. *Britons, Romans and Saxons around Salisbury and Cranborne Chase* 1948
F. S. Hinchy *The Heart of Dorset* 1953
J. Hutchins 3rd Ed *The History and Antiquities of the County of Dorset* 1861-1870
D. W. Insall & Associates *Blandford Forum – Conserve and Enhance* 1970
E. M. Leonard *The Early History of English Poor Relief* 1900
J. H. Lucking *Railways of Dorset* 1968
A. D. Mills *The Place-names of Dorset* Pt.ii 1980
J. Newman & N. Pevsner *The Buildings of Englnd (Dorset)* 1972
F. J. K. Penn *Historic Towns in Dorset* 1980
D. Popham *The Book of Wimborne* 1983
M. E. Rose *The English Poor Law (1780-1930)* 1971
Royal Commission on Historical Monuments Vol.iii 1970
R. R. Sellman *Illustrations of Dorset History* 1960
T. L. Stoate *Dorset Tudor Muster Rolls* 1978
T. Tribe & P. Whatmoor *Dorset Clocks and Clockmakers* 1981
C. Taylor *The Making of the English Landscape (Dorset)* 1970
S. & B. Webb *English Local Government* Vols. vii, viii, & ix
M. B. Weinstock *Old Dorset* 1967.

Index

Figures in *italics* refer to illustrations

Key to Caption Credits

DCM	Dorset County Museum (Shipp Collection)
DRO	Dorset County Record Office
SJ	Mr & Mrs S. Jardine
BM	Blandford Forum Museum Trust
JJH	J. J. Hobbs & Sons Ltd
DW	D. Waterman Esq